super-cute felt

35 step-by-step projects to make and give

LAURA HOWARD

CICO BOOKS

Acknowledgments

Many thanks to Cindy Richards for commissioning this book! I'm also hugely grateful to Pete, Sally, Kate, and the rest of the team at Cico Books for all the hard work they've put into this project.

Thanks to my family and friends for their kind words and encouragement throughout all my crafty endeavors. Special thanks to my mum for the constant support and for teaching me to sew all those years ago.

This edition published in 2017 by CICO Books

An imprint of Ryland Peters & Small Ltd
20–21 Jockey's Fields   341 E 116th St
London WC1R 4BW   New York, NY 10029

www.rylandpeters.com

10 9 8 7 6 5 4 3 2 1

First published in 2011 by CICO Books

Text © Laura Howard 2011
Design, illustration, and photography © CICO Books 2011

ISBN: 978 1 78249 460 7

Printed in China

Editor: Kate Haxell
Designer: Jacqui Caulton
Photographers: Emma Mitchell and Penny Wincer
Illustrator: Stephen Dew
Stylist: Sophie Martell

Contents

Introduction

Felt is awesome!

I've been sewing things with felt for as long as I can remember—my mom still has the felt apple I stitched for her in my first year of school. Felt crafting used to be thought of as just a simple hobby for kids learning to sew, but in recent years it's become hugely popular with crafters of all ages.

Felt is a really easy material to work with because it doesn't fray when cut. It's also perfect for making small projects that are quick to sew and don't require a huge outlay in materials. Most of the designs in this book can be made with the sheets or squares of felt that you can find in any craft store. If you don't have a craft or notions store near you, you can find an amazing range of colors and types of felt online, including 100 percent wool felt, eco-friendly felt, patterned felt, and fun supplies such as felt beads. There's more information on the different types of felt included in the materials section (page 6), and a list of suppliers is at the back of the book (page 128).

All the projects are hand-stitched—no sewing machine required! You also don't need any advanced sewing skills; the patterns use just a handful of basic stitches and all of these are explained in the techniques section (page 8), along with tips on working with felt.

If you're just learning to sew, or want a quick project for a rainy afternoon, try something small like one of the brooches (pages 14 and 30), the napkin rings (page 72), or an ornament (pages 100 and 104). The large designs like the tea cozy (page 76) and the cushion (page 82) are more time-consuming, but they're perfect for sewing gradually in the evenings in front of the television, and the finished result will be something you can be really proud of.

You can also adapt the designs in this book to suit you—use your favorite colors, resize the patterns to make them in custom sizes, or add more beads and sequins. Lots of the designs can also be personalized to make extra-special gifts.

If you're a confident crafter you can even mix-and-match motifs and projects to create new designs. For example, you could make brooches using a bumblebee, a cupcake, or the small toadstool; sew three pansies onto a lavender sachet; sew one peacock feather onto a headband; stitch clusters of forget-me-nots onto small backing pieces of felt to make pretty hair clips or barrettes; use the apple and pear motifs to make a pair of coasters; or use the cake stand design to decorate a cushion.

I hope this book gives you many happy hours of sewing!

Laura Howard

Materials

The primary material you are going to need is, of course, felt. There's a huge range of different felts available, but they can be divided into three main types.

Synthetic felt is the most widely available, and the type you'll probably find at your local craft store. The thickness and texture of this can vary depending on the range. You can also buy eco-friendly synthetic felt (made from recycled plastic), and patterned felt, which is printed with a pattern on the front and plain on the back.

Felt made from 100 percent wool has a lovely soft texture, and it's usually slightly thicker than standard synthetic felt. It's a luxurious option, making it perfect for special projects, and it usually comes in a range of softer and more "natural" looking colors than most standard synthetic ranges.

Wool blend felt contains a blend of wool and synthetic fibers—between 30–70 percent wool depending on the range. It's cheaper and thinner than 100 percent wool felt, but has a similar soft texture and wide range of colors.

I use all three types of felt in my crafting, and have used a mix throughout this book. If your felt is thin and the project you're making requires slightly stiffer or thicker felt (for example, to prevent a shape from flopping or to create a sturdy base for embroidery), you can just add an extra layer of felt to achieve the desired thickness.

Most felt can be gently hand washed, and some synthetic felt is even machine washable. Felt tends to "pill" or "bobble" slightly when washed (especially with frequent washing), and wool and wool blend felts will also shrink slightly. Check the packaging or with your supplier for washing instructions.

Almost all the projects in this book can be made with sheets or squares of craft felt, but for a couple of the larger designs you'll need to buy felt by the yard. For the hot water bottle cover (page 80) you will also need to make recycled felt from an old sweater. This is made by shrinking a woolen garment so the fibers contract and knit together, creating a thick fabric that can be cut without it unraveling. Use a 100 percent wool sweater—the thicker the sweater, the thicker the finished felt will be. Wash it at a high temperature in your washing machine with laundry detergent, and then tumble dry on a hot setting. You may need to repeat this to fully felt the sweater, and you may want to wash it inside a laundry bag to trap any fluff. The wool can shrink quite dramatically—make sure you use a large sweater to create a piece of felt big enough for the hot water bottle cover.

Two types of thread are used throughout this book.

Sewing thread, usually to match your chosen felt colors. Using matching threads helps the stitching become "invisible" on the finished piece. I often take small scraps of felt with me to the craft store so I can match colors as closely as possible.

Stranded cotton embroidery floss. This is made up of 6 or 8 strands that are easily divisible, so you can either sew with all the strands or separate off the number you want. The more strands you use, the larger the needle you'll need to use.

You will also need an assortment of embellishments and findings, as described in each project. Most of these are available from craft and notions stores, and packs of plain barrettes, hair clips, and headbands can also usually be acquired from your local jewelry shop.

Equipment

You don't need any special equipment to make the projects in this book; you'll probably already have most things at home.

A basic sewing kit of sewing scissors, needles (smaller ones for sewing thread, larger ones for embroidery floss), and pins.

A pair of embroidery scissors. Their small size makes cutting out little or intricate shapes much easier than with standard sewing scissors. You can buy them quite cheaply, and any type will do, but if you plan on cutting out lots of felt pieces I'd recommend buying a pair with comfortable handles.

A measuring tape, a ruler, scissors, and a pencil. You will also need a light-colored felt-tip pen if you want to draw the cushion (page 82) and notebook cover (page 52) patterns directly onto the back of the felt instead of making paper templates.

Greaseproof paper or thin tracing paper, for tracing embroidery patterns.

A wheel of long pins—these are larger and slightly thicker than dressmaker's pins. They're usually used for quilting, as they make it much easier to pin several layers of fabric together. You can get by without these pins, but they are very useful, especially for the larger projects.

I also used a pair of pinking shears (large scissors which cut a zigzag line) to trim the edges of some felt pieces for a nice decorative effect, but this is optional.

Techniques

Cutting out shapes

Photocopy the templates for your project from the back of the book, enlarging them to the required size, and carefully cut them out. Pin the paper templates to the felt you want to use. If the pieces are too small to pin, just hold the template in place between the thumb and forefinger of one hand while cutting around it with the other.

Roughly cut out the felt around the template so you're working with a smaller piece of felt, which will be much easier to maneuver. Then carefully cut out the shape, following the edge of the paper template, and turning the felt slowly as you work your way around the template.

Cutting out smaller or more intricate shapes

When cutting out very small shapes without a template, start by cutting out a small square of felt, then cut your shape out from the square using small, sharp embroidery scissors. To cut small circles, cut into the felt in a spiral motion, turning the felt around slowly as you cut (using your thumb as a pivot), and gradually making the spiral smaller until you get the size of circle you want. I find cutting in this spiral motion a good way to get a natural-looking curve on a very small circle.

I often cut two or three versions of a small shape before I get the one I'm happy with. Use leftover scraps of felt from other projects to practice cutting out the shape you want—fiddly jobs like this always get easier with practice.

If you're having difficulty cutting small shapes accurately freehand, try drawing the shape you want onto a piece of paper, cutting it out, and then using a small piece of clear adhesive tape to secure the paper template to a small square of felt. The tape will hold the paper in place while you cut out the shape from the felt.

Stitches

There are a few basic stitches that are used throughout this book.

Straight stitches

Pass the needle through to the front (pulling the thread completely through the felt), and then take it through to the back again, making one single stitch of the length required. You can use individual straight stitches decoratively, or sew a series of them to create simple patterns. Straight stitch is also used to sew one felt shape onto another (as pictured).

Running stitch

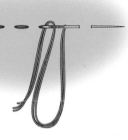

Pass the needle in and out in one step to create a row of even stitches, pulling the thread through the felt after each "in and out" (as pictured, left).

Alternatively, you can sew a line of small straight stitches (see above) to create the same effect. I usually do this when sewing through several layers of felt as I find it keeps my stitching neat.

Backstitch

Start with one straight stitch, then pass the needle through the felt a stitch length away from the end of the stitch, as if you're starting a second straight stitch. Instead of moving "forward" along the line you're sewing, sew back toward the first stitch and pass the needle through the felt as close to the end of the first stitch as possible, so they form a continuous line. Repeat this, each time starting your stitch a stitch length away from the previous stitch, and then sewing back to it.

Whip stitch

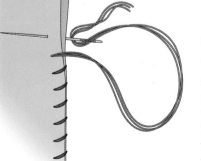

This is a slanting stitch used to sew two layers of felt together along their edges. Start the stitching between the two layers, so the knot is hidden, passing the needle through to the front. Sew a stitch that overlaps the edge at a slight diagonal angle, passing the needle through the felt at the back, and sewing through both layers of felt at another slight angle through to the front, so your needle comes out a short distance along from where you started. Repeat this to sew up the whole edge.

Blanket stitch

This is a decorative stitch used to sew two layers of felt together along their edges. Start the stitching between the two layers, so the knot is hidden, and pass the needle through to the front. Sew a stitch that overlaps the edge at a right angle, passing the needle through the felt at the back so it sews through both layers and emerges at the front exactly where it came out. Don't pull the thread completely through, but leave a small loop; pass the needle through this loop from the front to the back and pull it tight.

Begin the second stitch at the back of the felt, passing the needle through both layers so it emerges a short distance along the edge from the first stitch. Again, don't pull the thread completely through but leave a small loop, pass the needle through it from front to back and then pull it tight. Repeat this second stitch to sew along the whole edge.

Zigzags

Sew a series of straight stitches to create a zigzag line.

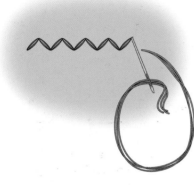

Stars

Sew four overlapping straight stitches to create a star shape. Start by sewing a cross of two stitches, then add the other two to complete the star.

Hearts

Sew a zigzag of four small stitches to create the top of the heart, then sew four more stitches in a "V" shape to complete it. It's important to make the stitches as even as possible so you don't end up with a lopsided heart.

Sewing on eyes

I've used several different techniques for sewing on small eyes and pupils—you can use the method described in each project, or stick to the one you find easiest.

Cut a small circle of black felt and sew it in place with either a cross or star of stitches in the center, or by straight stitching around the edges.

Use three strands of black embroidery floss to sew two or three small straight stitches close together, to create a very small eye. To stitch a larger eye, sew a small star of four overlapping stitches, then sew more stitches the same size on top (about eight of them) to fill in the gaps between the stitches, so you end up with a roughly circular shape.

Sew on a black seed bead using black sewing thread—sew the bead flat like an "O," using three or four stitches to hold it in place.

Sewing on ribbons

Use whip stitch to sew ribbon ties or loops in place, sewing along one edge of the ribbon where it overlaps the felt, and then back down the other edge. If possible, sew the whip stitches into the felt, hooking the needle into the fibers instead of passing it right the way through. By doing this you can secure the ribbon to the felt without the stitching being visible on the other side of the felt (the right side of the finished piece).

Sewing on findings

Use doubled sewing thread to sew on brooch clasps, sewing through each hole in the clasp several times to ensure a secure hold. Also use doubled thread and multiple stitches when sewing on other findings, such as barrettes, clips, and snap fasteners. To use a safety pin instead of a brooch clasp, cut a small rectangle of felt, place it over the fixed bar of the pin, and backstitch lines across it vertically and horizontally with doubled thread, until the pin is held firmly to the project.

To sew on lengths of elastic, or elastic headbands, use the same method as for sewing on ribbons—whip stitch along one side and then the other, sewing into the felt instead of through it.

Sewing on beads, buttons, and sequins

To sew on seed and bugle beads, use a fine needle and doubled sewing thread to match the felt you're sewing the beads to. One stitch should be sufficient to hold a small bead in place. To sew seed beads flat like an "O," use single thread and three or four stitches.

To sew sequins, use a fine needle and single sewing thread to match the sequins. Sew three evenly spaced stitches radiating out from the central hole to hold each sequin in place.

Sew buttons in position with doubled sewing thread to match the button or the backing felt, depending on the project. Sew through the holes several times to ensure the buttons are secure—the larger and heavier the button, the more stitches you will need. If the button has four holes, sew through them to create a cross shape.

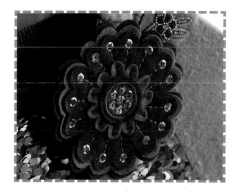

Stuffing

When making a design that requires stuffing, sew around most of the edge of the project, leaving a hole large enough to fit a finger or two through. Plan ahead for the best place to leave the hole—a flat surface at the bottom or side is usually best (you need to be able to poke stuffing into all the corners from this position).

Use toy stuffing to stuff the project, adding small pieces bit by bit and gradually filling up the shape. Start in the far corners, and use a pencil to poke the stuffing into all the corners and any narrow shapes. When you've added enough stuffing, squash the shape to even out the stuffing and remove any lumps. Then sew up the hole using the same stitching and thread as before.

The more stuffing you add to a shape, the denser the stuffing will become as it compresses. The denser the stuffing, the firmer your finished piece will be and the more rounded the shape you're stuffing will become (if overstuffed, the shape can become distorted). Most of the projects in this book just require light stuffing, so a three-dimensional shape is created, but the item remains very light and squashable.

Chapter 1
Accessories

bunny brooch

A sweet bunny rabbit to wear on your spring coat or cardigan. This rabbit brooch is made using appliquéd shapes with stitched details to give him a face full of character. Cutting out the small shapes requires a bit of patience (and felt that doesn't go fluffy at the edges), but the result is well worth it.

1 Using the templates, cut out one light brown body shape, two white tail shapes, one light pink left ear shape, and one light pink right ear shape. Also cut out two small circles from white felt for the eyes, and a small oval from light pink felt for the nose (see page 8 for techniques for cutting out small shapes).

2 Pin the body shape onto a backing piece of light green felt, leaving space all around the edge and room for the tail to stick out. Sew the bunny's body onto the backing felt using neat straight stitches in light brown thread, then remove the pin.

You will need:

Templates on page 110

Light brown felt, approx.
3 × 3in (8 × 8cm)

Light green felt, approx.
3½ × 7in (9 × 18cm)

Small pieces of light pink
and white felt

Matching sewing threads for all
felt colors, plus black thread

Needle, scissors, pins

Sew-on brooch finding

3 With light pink thread, carefully straight stitch the pink ear shapes in place in the center of the brown ears. Position the pink nose a tiny way in from the tip of the face and use more light pink thread to secure it with two small stitches in a cross in the center.

4 Place the two small white eyes on the face between the ears and the nose, and sew them in position with a small cross of white stitches in the center of each circle. Using the white thread, sew six small straight stitches radiating out from the nose (three on each side) to make the bunny's whiskers.

5 With more white thread, straight stitch both tail shapes in place at once, sewing one on top of the other to make an extra fluffy tail.

6 Using black sewing thread, sew small stitches in a curved line to "draw" a smiling mouth with the thread. Then sew lots of small black stitches on top of each other in the center of the eyes to form the pupils. Keep sewing stitch over stitch until you've made a solid black circle of thread in the center of each eye.

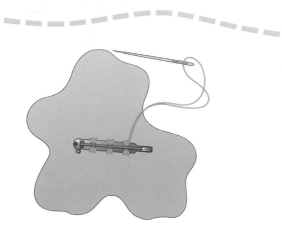

7 Cut around the bunny, leaving a narrow green border all around the edge and leaving extra felt between the ears and the body, as in the photograph (this will help make the brooch sturdier). Pin the bunny to more light green felt and use it as a template to cut out an identical backing piece.

8 Remove the pin and set aside the front of the brooch. Turn the plain backing piece over and sew a brooch finding securely to the center with doubled light green thread.

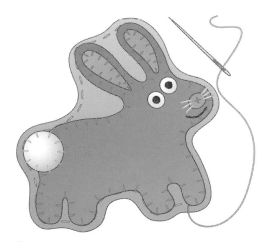

9 Pin the front of the brooch to the backing piece and sew them together with running stitch around the edge in light green thread. Follow the outline of the bunny wherever possible to help hide the stitches, and finish the thread neatly on the back.

pansy hair clips Pansies are one of my favorite flowers. These pansy hair clips are quick and easy to sew— make pairs as gifts, or make lots in different colors and wear a whole bouquet in your hair. You could also make pansy brooches by sewing a small brooch finding to the back instead of a hair clip.

1 Cut out all the petal shapes using the templates provided. Use a mix of purple and white for purple pansies, and a mix of sunny yellow and purple for yellow pansies. Cut pieces 4, 5, and 6 from the main color, piece 3 from a second color, piece 2 from a third color, and piece 1 from yellow felt. Cut a second piece 6 in the same color as the first one.

You will need:

Templates on page 110

Yellow, purple, lilac, and white felt, approx. 4½ × 5in (11 × 13cm) of the main color used for each flower, and small pieces of the other colors

Matching yellow and purple sewing threads and black sewing thread

Snap hair clip finding

Needle, scissors, pins

2 Arrange all the petal shapes (pieces 1–5) as pictured, on top of one of the backing shapes (piece 6). With yellow sewing thread, sew a small cross of two stitches in the middle of the small yellow central shape (piece 1). Sew through all the layers to hold them together.

3 Sew a series of black stitches radiating out from the center— six stitches at the top (three each side), and four at the bottom. Make sure you don't stitch over the edge of the backing piece as you sew.

4 Open a snap hair clip and sew the second, undecorated backing shape (piece 6) on top. Use doubled sewing thread and ensure the clip is pointing in the direction you want. If you're making a pair of pansy clips, make sure you sew one clip facing right and one facing left.

5 Place the pansy on top of the clip so the backing shapes line up neatly and sew them together. Use matching thread and carefully whip stitch around the edge, folding the pansy petals forward as you sew past them to ensure you don't catch them in the stitches. Finish the stitching neatly on the back.

kitty purse

Cat fans of all ages will love this cute kitty purse. Use it as a coin purse or add a length of ribbon to make a shoulder bag for a little girl. The purse has a fish on one side and a happy kitty on the other—you can customize the design to make the kitty into a portrait of your own cat.

1 Use the templates to cut out the following: four bright pink purse pieces, one orange fish, one black kitty face, one gray fur piece, two white eyes, two black pupils, one pink nose, and two pink ears. Into two of the purse pieces, cut the opening indicated by the dotted line on the template: these will be the purse back. Also cut out a very small black felt circle for the fish's eye, or use a small black bead instead (see page 8 for tips on cutting out small shapes).

2 Pin the orange fish to one of the back purse pieces, in the center of the space below the opening. Sew around the edge of the fish with straight stitch in matching orange sewing thread, then remove the pin. Use black sewing thread to sew on a small black circle or black bead for the fish's eye, and backstitch a curved line for the smile.

3 Cut a length of dark orange embroidery floss and separate half the strands (so for six-stranded floss, use three strands), and change to a larger needle if necessary. Using backstitch, sew three lines on the tail fin. Set aside the back purse pieces until later.

4 Pin the black kitty face to the center of one of the front purse pieces. Use straight stitch in black sewing thread to sew the face in position, then remove the pins. Next, appliqué the small pieces to the face using straight stitch and matching threads—first the patch of fur, then the eyes, pupils, ears, and nose.

5 Switch to a larger needle and, using half the strands of floss as before, embroider whiskers and a smile onto the cat. Backstitch a pink smiling mouth and three white lines on either side of the face, sewing the whiskers so they overlap the face onto the bright pink background.

You will need:

Templates on pages 110–111

Bright pink felt, approx. 9½ × 14½in (24 × 36cm)

Black felt, approx. 4 × 5in (10 × 13cm)

Small pieces of orange, pink, white, and gray felt

Matching sewing threads

White, pink, and dark orange stranded embroidery flosses (threads)

A bright pink zipper, 4in (10cm) long

Optional: ribbon, approx. ⅜in (1cm) wide, 25½in (65cm) long

Needles, scissors, pins

Customizing the cat

To create pattern pieces for your own cat's markings, draw around the cat face template onto paper and draw any markings on your cat's face onto it. Cut the shapes out and use them as templates to cut the right pieces from felt. Sew your custom shapes on in Step 4 instead of the patch of gray fur.

6 Place the two back pieces together, with the fish facing toward you. Arrange the zipper between the layers so it's positioned in the center of the opening and carefully pin the zipper in place (pinning through the zipper tape and both layers of felt). Test that the zipper opens easily and reposition it if necessary.

7 Use bright pink thread and neat running stitch to sew around the opening, sewing the zipper in place. Turn it over and back again as you sew to ensure the line of stitching is completely straight. Remove the pins and then sew back around the opening, filling in the gaps between the stitches to create a continuous line.

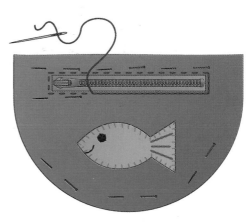

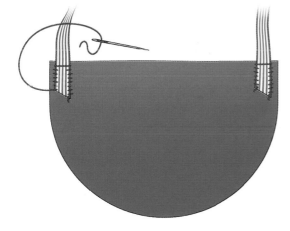

8 If you want to add a shoulder strap to the purse, cut a piece of pretty pink ribbon about 25½in (65cm) long, or the size you require. With the ends overlapping the felt by about ¾in (2cm), sew the ribbon to the top of the undecorated purse front piece with whip stitches in bright pink thread.

9 Pin all four layers of the purse together, so that the cat and fish both face outward and the ribbon ends are sandwiched between the two purse front pieces. Sew around the edges with blanket stitch in bright pink thread, stitching all the layers together. Hide the knots between the outer and inner layers and finish the stitching very neatly on the back.

feather headband

Wear a feather in your hair with this pretty headband. I used pale colors for a soft, romantic look, and added sparkle to the gray with silver embroidery floss. White and silver would have a similar effect, as would a soft brown with gold floss. If you prefer something more tropical, try using bright colors.

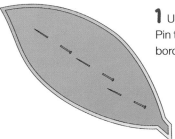

1 Using the template, cut out a feather shape from light gray felt. Pin this shape to the pale purple felt and cut around it, leaving a narrow border, so you have a purple feather slightly larger than the gray one.

2 With dark thread (to contrast clearly with the light felt) sew a slightly curved line of large running stitches down the center of the gray feather, finishing the stitches loosely so they can be easily removed. This line marks the center of the feather during the next step.

You will need:

Template on page 111

Light gray felt, approx.
4 × 7½in (10 × 19cm)

Light purple felt, approx.
8 × 8¾in (20 × 22cm)

Light purple sewing thread

Dark sewing thread

Silver stranded embroidery
floss (thread)

Elastic headband or
narrow elastic

Needles, scissors, pins

3 Cut out an assortment of narrow triangles along each side of the gray feather, pointing downward. Vary the lengths and placement of the triangles to create a natural-looking broken edge, and avoid cutting right up to or through the stitched line. When you're happy with how the feather looks, remove the guideline of stitches.

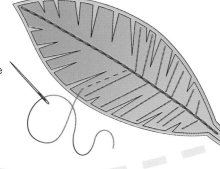

4 Pin the gray feather in the center of the purple backing feather. Cut a length of silver embroidery floss and separate half the strands (so for six-stranded floss, use three strands). Metallic embroidery floss can be a little harder to work than other flosses, so use short lengths to avoid tangling. Using a large needle, backstitch a slightly curved line down the center of the feather, sewing the gray and purple layers together and removing the pins as you sew.

5 Using single strands of the silver embroidery floss, sew one or two lines between each cut-out triangle. Sew neat running stitches from the center of the gray feather out toward the edge (almost up to but not touching the edge), and then sew back toward the center again, filling in the gaps to create a continuous line. Repeat this until the feather is covered with narrow stitched lines, securing the threads on the back.

6 Pin the feather to some more light purple felt and use it as a template to cut a matching backing shape. Remove the pins and set aside the backing shape.

7 If you're using a plain elastic headband, cut off the metal holding the loop together (or just cut the band if it's one continuous loop), and pin an end to either end of the feather. The elastic should overlap the feather as much as possible while still fitting your head. If you're using narrow sewing elastic, cut a piece the appropriate length. Whip stitch up one side of the elastic and back down the other, sewing into only the purple felt so that the stitches do not show on the front of the feather.

8 Add the backing shape, pinning it to the back of the feather to cover the workings and the ends of the elastic. Whip stitch around the edge with more light purple thread, removing the pins as you sew and finishing the stitches neatly on the back.

dachshund cuff

Is there a cuter dog than the dachshund? This extra-long sausage dog will spend many happy hours chasing its own tail round your wrist. I love the yellow and turquoise color combination, and the darker turquoise prevents the workings of the embroidery flosses showing through the yellow felt.

1 Using the templates, cut out a brown dog and a dark brown ear. For the background, cut one yellow and one turquoise rectangle, each measuring 2 x 6in (5 x 15cm).

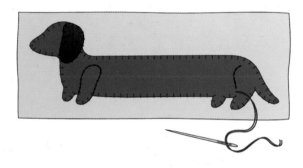

2 Pin the dachshund to the center of the yellow cuff piece, and sew around the edge with straight stitch in brown sewing thread. Sew the ear in place with straight stitch in dark brown sewing thread. Then use doubled dark brown thread to backstitch lines marking the shapes of the legs on the dog's body, using the dotted lines on the template as a guide.

You will need:

Templates on page 111

Brown felt, approx.
2½ × 6in (6 × 15cm)

Small piece of dark
brown felt

Yellow felt, approx.
2¾ × 6¾in (7 × 17cm)

Turquoise felt, approx.
2¾ × 6¾in (7 × 17cm)

Brown, dark brown,
black, turquoise, and yellow
sewing threads

Purple, turquoise, and
black stranded embroidery
flosses (threads)

Black seed bead

Black elastic, ¼in (5mm)
wide, approx. 4in (10cm) long

Needles, scissors, pins

3 Cut a length of black embroidery floss and separate half the strands (so for six-stranded floss, use three strands). Switch to a larger needle if necessary and sew a few stitches close together to form the dog's nose. Use black sewing thread to backstitch a curved line to form the smile, and sew on a black seed bead for the eye. Sew the bead in place with three or four stitches, sewing it flat like an "O."

4 Fill in the empty space around the dachshund with small embroidered turquoise and purple stars. Use half the strands of embroidery floss (as before), and sew four overlapping stitches to create each eight-pointed star.

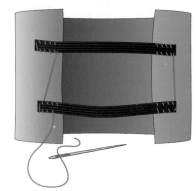

5 Cut two lengths of black elastic, each approximately 2in (5cm) long. To make a larger or smaller cuff, cut enough elastic to make the cuff fit your wrist, plus an extra ¾in (2cm) to allow for the elastic to be sewn to the felt. Sew the elastic to the turquoise cuff piece, positioning it so it overlaps the felt by about ⅜in (1cm) at each end and whip stitching it in place with turquoise sewing thread. Sew both lengths of elastic to one end of the cuff and then fold the cuff around to make a circle so you can sew the elastic to the other end.

6 Sew the decorated yellow cuff piece onto the turquoise cuff piece, sandwiching the ends of the elastic between them. Pin the layers together with the turquoise felt on the inside and sew the edges together with blanket stitch in yellow sewing thread. Finish the stitching neatly on the inside of the cuff.

retro corsage

This large flower brooch was inspired by the floral patterns found on vintage fabrics and wallpapers. Wear it on your coat to chase the winter blues away, or sew a barrette or an elastic headband onto the back instead of a brooch and wear it in your hair for parties.

1 Use the templates to cut out all the pieces. From magenta felt cut out corsage 1, corsage 3, center 2, and two corsage back pieces. From coral felt cut out corsage 2, center 1, and center 3. You'll end up with pieces that, when sewn together, alternate between the two colors.

You will need:

Templates on page 112

Magenta felt, approx.
8 × 9in (20 × 23cm)

Coral or orange felt, approx.
4¾ × 7½in (12 × 19cm)

22 pink sequins, approx.
¼in (5mm) diameter

Pink and purple sewing threads

Pink and magenta stranded
embroidery flosses (threads)

Brooch finding

Needles, scissors, pins

2 Layer the largest four pieces on top of each other (corsages 1, 2, and 3 and center 3) as pictured. Cut a length of pink embroidery floss and separate half the strands (so for six-stranded floss, use three strands). Using a large needle, sew the four pieces together with a cross of two small stitches in the center. Then sew lines radiating out from the edge of the central coral shape, using running stitch to sew out toward the edge of the petals and back again to create a continuous line of stitching. Sew three lines on each of the five petals, sewing through all three layers but only stitching up to approximately ¼–⅜in (5–10mm) away from the tips of the first layer of petals.

3 With pink sewing thread, sew one pink sequin to the end of each line of stitching. The sequins should overlap the end of the stitched lines and be sewn in place with three stitches per sequin. To keep the back of the corsage as neat as possible, start the stitching at the center of the corsage and sew up the back toward each sequin, and then back toward the center.

4 Sew one of the corsage back pieces to the back of the flower, positioning it in the middle and securing it with a small cross of two pink stitches. Then position the two center circles (centers 1 and 2) in the middle of the front flower, covering the cross. Cut a length of magenta embroidery floss and separate half the strands, as before. Hold the center circles on the front of the flower between your thumb and forefinger and backstitch a magenta line around the edge of the smallest circle, sewing through all the layers.

5 Using three stands of magenta floss, sew one stitch on each of the small coral petals surrounding the center circles. Make sure you don't sew over the edge of the backing circle as you do this.

6 Arrange seven pink sequins inside the magenta backstitch circle, sewing one sequin in the center and the rest in a circle around it. Use pink sewing thread and sew each sequin in place with three stitches.

7 Sew the brooch finding to the remaining back piece, sewing it slightly above the center of the circle using doubled purple sewing thread. Then place the backing circle on the circle sewn to the back of the flower and whip stitch them together with purple thread. Finish the stitches neatly on the back.

bird on a branch necklace

This fun statement necklace features a little brown bird perched on a leafy branch— a great accessory to wear with your favorite dress in spring or summer. You could also make an autumnal version with orange and red leaves. I used ribbon ties for the necklace, but you could swap these for the cord and clasp from an old necklace.

1 Using the templates, cut out one dark brown branch, one mid-brown little bird, one light brown little bird wing, and four large and five small bright spring-green leaves.

2 Pin the branch onto a piece of light blue felt, leaving plenty of room to add the bird and leaves later. Straight stitch around the edge of the branch with dark brown sewing thread and remove the pins.

3 Arrange the leaves as pictured and pin them on. Sew around the edge of each leaf with matching green thread and neat straight stitches, removing the pins as you sew. Then use doubled thread to backstitch a line down the center of each leaf.

4 Pin the bird to the branch. The necklace is designed to be hung so the tip of the top leaf on the left and the end of the branch on the right are level with each other—use this as a guide to position the bird. Use matching threads to straight stitch the bird in position. Then straight stitch the light brown wing to the body.

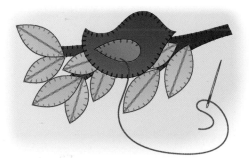

5 Cut lengths of mid-brown and light brown floss and set aside half the strands (so for six-stranded floss, use three strands). Switch to a larger needle if necessary and add details to the wing and body. Sew small single stitches on the tummy with light brown thread. On the wing, sew rows of "V" shapes with mid-brown thread.

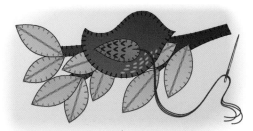

You will need:

Templates on page 112

Light blue felt, approx.
7 × 8in (18 x 20cm)

Bright spring-green felt,
approx. 3½ × 4⅓in (9 × 11cm)

Dark brown felt, approx.
2 × 6in (5 × 15cm)

Mid-brown felt, approx.
2½ × 3in (6 × 8cm)

Small pieces of light brown,
black, and white felt

Matching sewing threads

Mid- and light brown stranded
embroidery flosses (threads)

Light blue ribbon,
approx. ¼in (5mm) wide,
32in (80cm) long

Needles, scissors, pins

6 Cut a small circle from white felt and a very small circle from black. These will be the eye and pupil. (See page 8 for tips on cutting out small shapes: if you have difficulties cutting the pupil, use a black bead or sew small black stitches on top of each other in the center of the eye). Sew on the eye and pupil with straight stitches in matching sewing thread.

7 Trim the excess blue felt from around the necklace leaving a border of at least ¼in (5mm) all the way around, as pictured. Use this as a template to cut out a matching shape from more light blue felt to use as the backing piece for the necklace.

8 Cut two 16in (40cm) lengths of light blue ribbon. Sew the ribbons to the top of the backing piece at the far left and right, using whip stitches in matching thread. The ribbon should overlap the felt by about ⅜in (1cm). Trim the ends of the ribbons at an angle to help prevent fraying.

9 Pin the front and back pieces of the necklace together and sew the edges together with whip stitch in blue thread. Hide the knots between the two layers and finish the stitches neatly on the back.

sewing brooch Love sewing? Show off your love for all things notions-related with this cute sewing-themed brooch. This project is a great way to use up odd buttons in your sewing box, and would make a sweet gift for a crafty friend.

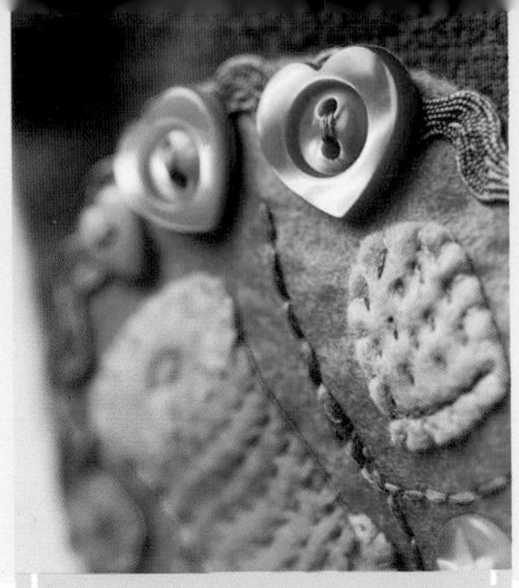

1 Use the templates to cut out two orange background oval pieces, one turquoise thread piece, one gray thimble piece, and two light brown spool pieces. Arrange all the small pieces on one of the orange ovals, as pictured, positioning the turquoise thread piece so it overlaps the bottom spool piece. Baste all the pieces in place with large stitches in black thread, finishing the stitches very loosely so you can easily unpick them later.

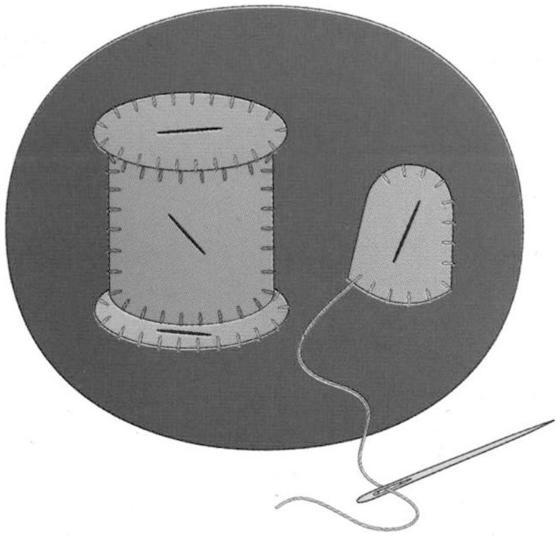

2 Sew all the pieces in position with matching sewing thread, sewing around the edges of each shape with straight stitches. Remove the large black basting stitches.

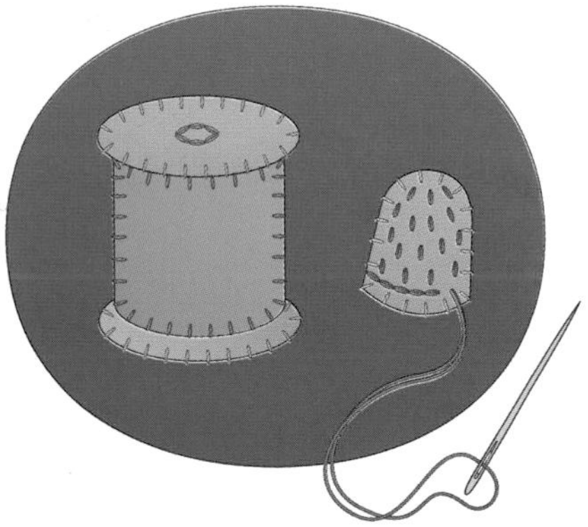

3 With doubled light brown sewing thread, backstitch a small oval in the center of the top of the spool to represent the hole. Then use doubled gray sewing thread to sew a series of small stitches to represent the dimples on the thimble, and sew a curved backstitch line close to the bottom of the thimble.

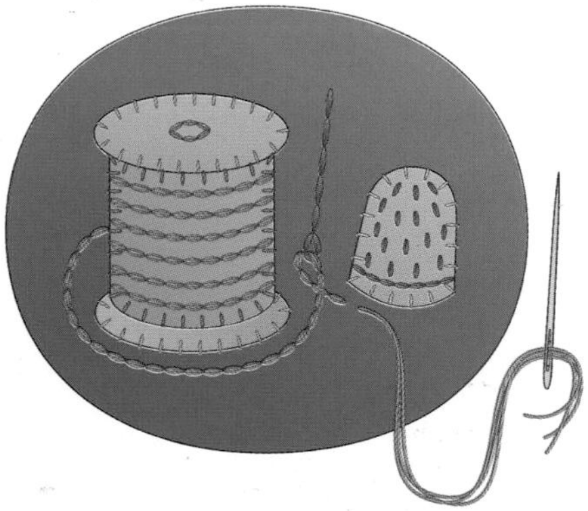

4 Switch to a larger needle and gray embroidery floss to backstitch a sewing needle shape in the center of the brooch. Work a couple of extra stitches at the bottom to create the eye of the needle. Then cut a length of turquoise embroidery floss and separate half the strands (so for six-stranded floss, use three strands). Use these to backstitch a series of curved lines across the turquoise thread shape, and then a long, curved line around the spool and through the eye of the gray needle, as pictured.

You will need:

Templates on page 113

Orange felt, approx. 4 × 6¼in (10 × 16cm)

Small pieces of turquoise, gray, and light brown felt

Matching sewing threads

Black sewing thread

Turquoise and gray stranded embroidery flosses (threads)

Assorted small buttons

Purple rickrack, ¼in (5mm) wide, 14in (35cm) long

Needles, scissors, pins

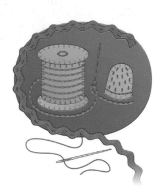

5 Sew rickrack to the edge of the oval with purple thread, using short stitches and curving it to fit. The rickrack should overlap the edge slightly so only a small amount of orange can be seen around the edge. When you've sewn all the way around, trim excess rickrack and sew a few stitches over the end.

6 Arrange a selection of buttons on the brooch, filling in the gaps and using one button to cover the join in the rickrack border. Make a note of which buttons you want where, and one by one sew them in place using doubled purple sewing thread.

7 Sew the brooch finding to the back of the plain oval with doubled orange sewing thread. Pin the backing oval to the decorated front oval and sew them together. Use purple sewing thread and sew running stitches around the rickrack border, making sure the stitching on the back is as neat as possible.

butterfly & flower barrettes

A pair of pretty barrettes for a touch of summer in your hair, whatever the weather. These would be lovely to wear for parties or weddings, perhaps even made to match a wedding scheme and worn by bridesmaids. Make a mismatched pair as pictured, or add butterflies to both barrettes.

You will need:

Templates on page 113

Mint-green felt, approx.
6¼ × 7in (16 × 18cm)

Light pink felt, approx.
4 × 5in (10 × 13cm)

Small pieces of lilac,
pale purple, and pale pink felt

Lilac, light pink, and mint-green
sewing threads

Lilac, light pink, and silver
stranded embroidery
flosses (threads)

2 plastic hair barrettes,
approx. 2¾in (7cm) wide

Needles, scissors, pins

1 For each barrette you want to make, use the templates to cut out three light pink flowers, two mint-green base pieces, and four mint-green leaves —one of each of the four leaf shapes provided.

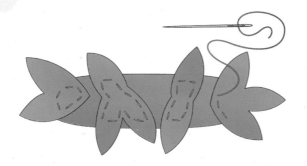

2 Arrange the leaf shapes on one of the base pieces as shown (from left to right, leaves 1–4), and sew them in place with green sewing thread and running stitch. When sewing the leaves and other details to the base, avoid sewing right up to or over the edges of the base piece.

3 Position the three pink flowers on top of the leaves. For flower-only barrettes, space the flowers evenly with the middle flower on top so it slightly overlaps the others (as shown). For barrettes with a butterfly, move the middle flower across a little to leave a gap on the side you want the butterfly. Sew the flowers in place with light pink sewing thread and a small cross of two stitches in the center of each flower. Secure any overlapped petals with small stitches to hold them in place under the overlapping middle flower.

4 Cut a length of pink embroidery floss and separate two strands. Use these to sew ten stitches radiating out from the center of each flower—one long stitch down the center of each petal, and one short stitch between each petal. Start the sewing away from the center of the flowers, so the floss knot isn't in the middle and won't keep getting caught by the needle.

5 Cut one very small circle from pale pink felt for each flower (see page 8 for techniques for cutting out small shapes). Place one circle in the center of each flower and sew it in place with a single strand of silver embroidery floss. Sew a small star of four overlapping stitches in the center of the circle, then sew small stitches radiating out from the circle, sewing one stitch between each pink stitch sewn in Step 4. If you have trouble cutting out the felt circles you could sew a pink or silver seed bead into the center of each flower instead.

6 Using the butterfly templates, cut out one small butterfly wings from pale purple felt, and one large butterfly wings and one body piece from lilac felt. Place the small butterfly wings on top of the large wings and hold them together. Backstitch around the edge of the small shape with lilac embroidery floss, sewing the two layers together. Begin and end the stitching on the center back of the butterfly, so the knots will be completely hidden when you sew the butterfly onto the barrette.

7 With two strands of silver embroidery floss, fill the space inside the embroidered lilac lines with slightly curving horizontal lines of backstitching. Start and finish sewing on the center back of the butterfly, as before, so the knots will be hidden.

8 Put the butterfly body piece on top of the butterfly wings and arrange the butterfly in the gap between the flowers. Sew the butterfly in position, sewing around the body with running stitch in lilac sewing thread and then around again, and so filling in the gaps to create a continuous line of stitching.

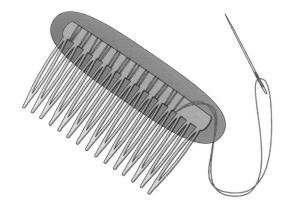

9 Take the second, undecorated, base piece and hold it against the front of the hair barrette. Turn the barrette over, still holding the felt in place, and carefully sew the felt onto the barrette using doubled green sewing thread. Sew between the teeth of the barrette, sewing two stitches between each tooth and starting and finishing the stitching at the front, so the workings will be hidden when the barrette is finished.

10 Place the decorated front and plain back base pieces together and turn the barrette over so the flowers are facing away from you. Whip stitch around the edge of the base pieces with green thread. Finish the stitches neatly on the back of the barrette.

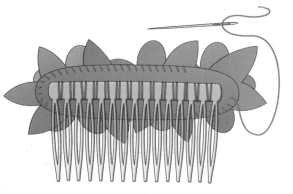

Chapter 2
Gifts

hedgehog phone case

A friendly hedgehog to help protect your phone against bumps and scratches. This case should fit most smart phones, but you can resize the pieces for a custom fit. When your phone is placed centrally on the back piece there should be a felt border approximately ⅜in (1cm) wide all around it.

1 Use the templates to cut one hedgehog body from light brown felt, one hedgehog spikes piece from dark brown felt, and two phone case backs and two fronts from spring-green felt. Also cut out a small dark brown oval for the nose and a small black circle for the eye (see page 8 for techniques for cutting out small shapes).

2 Position the hedgehog body and spikes pieces as pictured, at the right-hand end of one of the front case pieces. Use one of the shorter back pieces as a guide to ensure the hedgehog will be in the center of the case when the flap is folded over. Pin the body and spikes in place.

You will need:

Templates on page 114

Spring-green felt, approx. 10⅝ × 12in (27 × 30cm)

Dark brown felt, approx. 3 × 4in (8 × 10cm)

Light brown felt, approx. 2¾ × 4½in (7 × 11cm)

Small piece of black felt

Matching sewing threads

Leaf-green and light brown stranded embroidery flosses (threads)

Two snap fasteners

Needles, scissors, pins

3 Sew around the spikes with straight stitches in dark brown sewing thread. Then remove the pins and sew around the hedgehog's face and feet with straight stitches in light brown sewing thread.

4 Use straight stitches in matching sewing threads to sew the nose and eye in position on the hedgehog's face. Then use black sewing thread to backstitch a curved line to form the smile.

5 Cut light brown embroidery floss and separate half the strands (so for six-stranded floss, use three strands). Use these strands, and a larger needle if necessary, to sew lots of single straight stitches on the brown spikes. Start at the face and work across the dark brown felt, making each stitch about the same length.

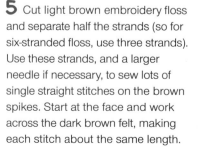

6 Using doubled green sewing thread, sew the stud halves of the snap fasteners to one end of a back phone case piece, positioning them approximately 1in (2.5cm) in from each edge.

7 Place all four phone case pieces on top of each other, starting with the decorated front piece with the hedgehog facing downward, then the plain front piece, then the plain back piece, and then the back piece with the snap fasteners on top. Line up the edges as neatly as possible and pin the layers together.

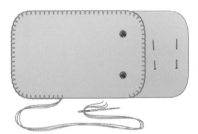

8 Cut a length of leaf-green embroidery floss and separate half the strands. Blanket stitch the short ends of the two back pieces together (where the case opening will be), hiding the knot between the layers. Sew across the ends and when you reach the other side, start sewing through all four layers to sew down the side, along the bottom and back up the other side. The phone case should now be sewn together except for the top flap.

9 Remove the pins. Fold over the top flap and press it onto the studs of the snaps to make dents in the felt. Use these marks to position the other halves of the fasteners on the top flap. Sew them to the inner layer only with doubled green sewing thread. Make a couple of stitches, fold over the flap to check you're sewing the snaps on in the right place, then sew them on securely.

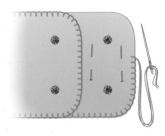

10 Pin the two flap pieces together and continue the green embroidery floss blanket stitching round the flap, finishing the stitching neatly inside the case.

Hedgehog Phone Case **39**

bumblebee lavender sachet

These scented sachets are inspired by the wobbly way bumblebees fly around lavender plants in the summer—if you've ever grown lavender in your yard you'll know how much bees love it! As well as smelling lovely, lavender sachets are a great chemical-free way to keep moths away from your out-of-season wool coats and sweaters.

You will need:

Templates on page 114

Light purple felt, approx. 4¾ × 9½in (12 × 24cm) for each sachet

Small pieces of bright yellow, black, and white felt

Matching sewing threads

Black stranded embroidery floss (thread)

Needles, scissors, pins

Teaspoon

Dried lavender

1 Cut out two squares measuring 4 x 4in (10 x 10cm) from light purple felt. Cut out the bee body template and carefully cut along the dotted lines to create six small paper strips. You can decorate the sachet with one bee or a pair of bees—for each bee, carefully cut out two white wing shapes and alternating black and yellow felt stripes (as pictured).

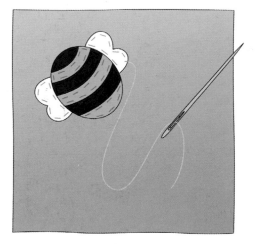

2 Arrange the bee pieces on one of the purple squares. You will sew them to the second purple square, transferring the pieces one by one to sew them in place. Alternate between black and yellow sewing thread to sew the stripes—using a line of running stitch along each side of every stripe. Use white thread and a line of running stitches around the edge to sew each wing in position.

3 Cut a length of black embroidery floss and set aside half the strands (so for six-stranded floss, use three strands). You may need to switch to a slightly larger needle if yours has a small eye. Use the embroidery floss to sew the bee's antennae. Each antenna consists of one small straight stitch at an angle from the front of the bee's body, topped with a small cross of two stitches.

4 With more black embroidery floss (using half the strands, as before), sew a line of stitches to form a trail where each bee has flown. Make the stitches as even as possible and sew curving lines and loops, stopping just before you reach the edge of the purple square. For sachets with two bees, stitch one flight line for each bee.

5 Sew the decorated front to the plain back with running stitch in purple sewing thread. Start on the inside (so the knot is hidden) ¾in (2cm) from a corner. Sew around the edge, leaving a gap to insert the teaspoon. Then sew back along the line, sewing in the spaces between stitches to create a continuous line. Spoon lavender into the sachet, using the handle to poke grains into the corners to ensure the sachet is evenly filled. Sew up the gap with purple thread, stitching along and then back as before to form a continuous line. Finish the stitches neatly on the back.

fruity pincushion & needlebook

Brighten up your sewing box with this matching needlebook and pincushion set. I chose vivid turquoise and candy-pink to contrast with the bright red and spring-green of the apple and pear, and coordinated the rickrack and needlebook pages with my color scheme, but you can use any colors you like.

The pincushion

1 Using the templates, cut out two turquoise circles (these will be the top and bottom of the pincushion), one red outer apple shape, and one white inner apple shape. Cut one long turquoise rectangle (this will be the sides), measuring 1¾ x 10in (4.5 x 25cm).

2 Position the outer apple shape slightly off-center on one of the circles, so that when the stalk and leaf are added, the whole apple is centered on the circle.

3 With matching sewing thread and straight stitches, sew the outer apple shape to the circle. Place the white inner apple shape in the center of the outer and use white sewing thread to straight stitch it in place. With more white thread, sew a line of backstitch down the center of the fruit.

4 Carefully cut out five small teardrop-shaped pips and a slightly curved stalk from dark brown felt, and one small leaf shape from green felt. Cut the bottom of the stalk into a "V" so it will fit neatly into the shape of the top of the apple.

5 Use dark brown sewing thread to straight stitch the stalk at the top of the fruit. Position the pips radiating outward, two one side of the backstitch line and three the other. Backstitch down the center of each pip with brown thread. Position the leaf as if it's growing from the bottom of the stalk, and backstitch down the center of it with green sewing thread.

6 Wrong sides facing, hold the decorated circle and a long edge of the rectangle together, and whip stitch them with turquoise sewing thread, gradually turning the circle as you sew the rectangle to it. Trim any excess overlapping felt from the rectangle once you have sewn it around the circle.

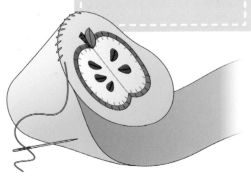

7 Cut a length of rickrack ¾in (2cm) longer than the circumference of the pincushion. Using red thread and a line of straight stitches down the middle of the rickrack, carefully sew it in place around the side of the pincushion so the rickrack overlaps the ends of the rectangle by ⅜in (1cm) at each end.

8 Sew up the side seam of the pincushion with turquoise thread using whip stitches, and tucking in the loose ends of the rickrack as you sew.

9 Turn the pincushion upside down and whip stitch the bottom circle to the long edge of the rectangle, as in Step 6. Use more turquoise thread and leave a gap for stuffing the pincushion.

10 Stuff the pincushion with polyester filling, or use small scraps of felt and/or fabric for a firmer, heavier pincushion. Sew up the gap with turquoise whip stitches and finish the sewing neatly on the bottom of the pincushion.

The needlebook

11 Using the templates, cut out one green outer pear shape and one white inner pear shape. Cut two pink rectangles and two green rectangles, each measuring 3½ x 6in (9 x 15cm).

12 Position the green pear shape in the center of the right-hand side of one of the pink rectangles. Follow Steps 3–5 to appliqué the pear pieces, but leave the end of the stalk straight so that it sits neatly on top of the inner pear shape.

13 Trim the edges of both green rectangles with pinking shears. Place the green rectangles on top of each other, and position them in the center of the undecorated pink rectangle. Pin them in place, then sew two lines of backstitch down the center using green thread. Finish the stitches on the back of the pink rectangle.

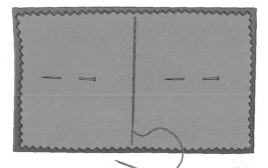

14 For the needlebook ties, cut two 8in (20cm) pieces of narrow pink ribbon, cutting the ends at an angle to help prevent fraying. Sew a length of ribbon in place in the middle of each short edge of the needlebook, on the back of the rectangle with the green "pages". The ribbon should overlap the rectangle by ¾in (2cm) and be sewn on neatly with whip stitches in pink thread—make the back of the stitching as neat as possible as it will be visible inside the needlebook.

15 Pin the two pink rectangles together so the green pages and the appliquéd pear both face outward, and the sewn-on ribbon ends are sandwiched between the pieces. Use pink thread to blanket stitch around the edges, sewing a couple of whip stitches where the ribbon ties emerge. Finish the stitches neatly inside the book.

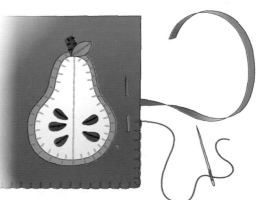

mug cozy

As well as keeping your drink hot and your hands cool, cozies are a great way to personalize a plain mug, and they make a great gift. I used 100 percent wool felt as it's thicker and tougher than standard craft felt and so it can be embroidered without puckering (with thinner felt use a double layer).

1 Cut two rectangles measuring 2⅞ x 9½in (7.5 x 24cm) from blue felt for the actual cozy. Using the templates, cut out three top cup shapes from white felt, three bottom cup shapes from white felt, and three tea shapes from light brown felt. Carefully cut a hole in the handle of each top cup shape: cut up along the side of the cup and stop just before you cut off the handle completely, then cut out a small "D" shaped piece to leave a narrow curved handle.

You will need:

Templates on page 115

Blue wool felt, approx.
7 × 10in (18 × 25cm)

White felt, approx. 4 × 8¼in
(10 × 21cm)

Small pieces of light brown felt

Matching sewing threads

White and blue stranded
embroidery flosses (threads)

Narrow blue ribbon,
8in (20cm)

Chunky blue button

Needles, scissors, pins

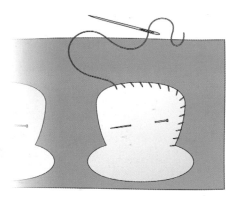

2 Position the three bottom cup pieces in a row along one of the blue cozy pieces, leaving room to sew on the button at one end and leaving space above the cups to add the embroidery. Pin them in place and sew around the edges with white sewing thread and straight stitches.

3 Place one top cup piece on each bottom cup piece, to give the effect of a cup sitting on a saucer. Pin them in place and sew them on with straight stitch in white sewing thread. Sew around the main cup shape first, then sew the loose end of the handle in place with a couple of stitches, and finally sew the handle in place with a series of straight stitches right across it.

4 Add a tea piece to each cup, sewing each one in place with straight stitch in light brown sewing thread.

5 Cut a length of white embroidery floss and separate half the strands (so for six-stranded floss, use three strands). Using a slightly larger needle if necessary, sew curving steam lines coming up from the tea. Use backstitch to create a continuous line, and make the lines as varied as possible with organic curves and loops. Repeat for all the cups.

6 Using three strands of blue embroidery floss, embroider details on to each cup. Backstitch a line around the inside of the saucer, a little way in from the edge, and two curved lines around the cup to create a band across it. Then sew small crosses (made from two stitches) and hearts (see page 10) inside the band. Repeat this for all three cups, varying the pattern slightly for each one.

7 Sew a button securely in place in the middle of one short edge of the cozy using doubled blue sewing thread.

8 Cut an 8in (20cm) length of narrow blue ribbon, cutting the ends at an angle to help prevent fraying. Sew ¾in (2cm) of one end to the backing cozy piece, on the opposite edge to the button but at the same height. Sew a line of neat stitches down the center of the ribbon and back again to attach it to the cozy. Finish the stitches on the ribbon side (the other side will be visible when the cozy is completed).

9 Wrong sides facing, pin the front and back pieces of the cozy together. Sew around the edges using matching sewing thread and neat blanket stitch, sewing a couple of whip stitches as you sew over where the ribbon emerges. Remove the pins as you sew and finish the stitches on the back. To fasten the cozy, wind the ribbon twice around the button. Slimmer mugs will need less ribbon, so trim any excess if necessary.

rainbow rosettes

Reward birthday boys and girls, best friends, or super moms with a prize rosette! These large rosettes can be personalized by adding a felt initial or number, or by embroidering a name or short message in the center circle. You can enlarge the templates to make a bigger rosette if you wish.

1 Using the templates, cut out three center circle shapes from one color, one star shape from another, and one ribbons shape from a third. If you're personalizing the rosette with a felt letter or number, make a template to fit within the center circle, leaving at least ¼in (5mm) clear around the edge of the circle.

2 Pin one of the circles to a contrasting bright color and cut a scalloped border around it. Then pin both layers to another color and cut more scallops, cutting each scallop between two previous scallops (the placing doesn't have to be exact for the effect to look great). Repeat this until you have six scalloped layers around the circle, each one a different color.

You will need:

Templates on page 115
8 sheets of felt in assorted bright colors, each 9 × 9in (23 × 23cm)
Matching sewing threads
Brooch finding
Needle, scissors, pins

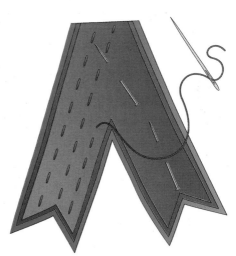

3 Pin the ribbon shape onto a contrasting bright color and cut a border around it to create a larger shape. The border should be equal all the way around except for across the top, which you should cut flush with the original ribbon shape. Repeat this with a third color. You can use the same colors for the ribbon layers as you used for the scallops, but make sure you use them in a different order to create different combinations of colors.

4 Sew the three ribbon pieces together with lines of running stitch in sewing thread matching the top color. Stitch three lines down each side of the ribbon.

5 Set aside one circle piece, and arrange the other pieces on top of each other. Place a circle at the bottom, then add the ribbons, then the scalloped layers, then a second circle on top with a star or the custom felt shape in the center. Line up the top and bottom circles as carefully as possible.

6 Holding all the pieces together, sew the star or felt letter in place with matching sewing thread. Use running stitch and sew around the edge of the star, or other shape, sewing through all the layers.

7 Sew a brooch finding onto the third circle using doubled matching sewing thread.

8 Place the third circle at the back of the rosette, matching the edges to the circle already there. Carefully stitch through all the layers, sewing a line of running stitch with matching thread around the edge of the circles. Make sure the line of stitching on the front is as neat as possible, and finish the stitches on the back.

under the sea notebook cover

Turn a plain notebook into a cute gift with this marine-theme cover. The cover is removable so it can be reused, and there's a storage pocket on the back. I used a 6⅛ × 8¾in (15.5 × 22cm) notebook—if your notebook is smaller or larger, resize all the sea life to suit.

You will need:

Templates on page 115

Turquoise felt, approx. 20 × 20in (50 × 50cm), plus 3½ × 3½in (9 × 9cm) for the pocket

Pink felt, approx. 2 × 2½in (5 × 6cm)

Orange felt, approx. 3 × 3in (8 × 8cm)

Small pieces of brightly colored felt

Matching sewing threads

Pink, black, and light orange stranded embroidery flosses (threads)

Tape measure, paper, pen, ruler, and adhesive tape

A hardback notebook

Greaseproof paper or thin tracing paper

Needles, scissors, pins

1 Use a tape measure to measure the outside cover of your notebook. Add ⅝in (1.5cm) to the height and 6in (15cm) to the width—to create a 3in (8cm) flap at each end. The measurements (including the added extra) for my notebook cover were 9¼ × 19in (23.5 × 48cm). Either make a large paper pattern from these measurements (join smaller pieces of paper together with adhesive tape to make one large piece), or draw them directly onto the back of the felt with a light-colored felt-tip pen. Cut out two identical pieces from turquoise felt. Also cut a 3 × 3in (8 × 8cm) square for the pocket.

2 Cut out the other pieces using the templates: a pink jellyfish, an orange starfish, and 11 or 12 little fish from an assortment of bright colors.

3 Pin the starfish to the center of the pocket. Cut a length of light orange embroidery floss and separate half the strands (so for six-stranded floss, use three strands). Using these strands and a large needle, sew around the edge of the starfish with small running stitches.

4 Place the two notebook cover pieces together and wrap them around the book, with the front ends folded inside the book's cover. This is to get a general idea of how the final item will look so that you can see where to position the jellyfish on the front cover. Arrange the jellyfish where you want it, then carefully unfold the felt from the book and pin the jellyfish to the outer layer only.

5 Cut a length of pink embroidery floss and separate half the strands, as before. Use these strands to sew around the jellyfish with backstitch, sewing a straight line along the bottom (just above the scalloped edge).

6 Trace the jellyfish embroidery pattern onto greaseproof paper or thin tracing paper. Line up the dotted line with the stitched line along the bottom of the jellyfish and pin the paper in place. Use more pink embroidery floss (half the strands, as before) to sew along the curved lines of the pattern in backstitch. Sew up to the bottoms of the felt scallops, taking care not to sew too tightly to avoid puckering the felt. Remove the pins and tear the paper away from the stitching carefully, using a pin to remove any remaining small pieces.

7 Cut a length of black embroidery floss and separate half the strands, as before. Use these strands to sew a few very small stitches close together to make the eyes of the starfish, and then to backstitch a curved smile. Repeat this to sew eyes and a smile on the jellyfish.

8 Wrap the notebook pieces around the book again (as in Step 4) and arrange a shoal of little fish on the front. Carefully remove the outer notebook layer and baste all the fish to it with one long stitch in the center of each fish. Use black sewing thread and finish the stitches loosely so you can easily unpick them. Backstitch around the edge of each fish with matching sewing threads. When you've sewn on all the fish, remove the black stitches.

9 Use more black embroidery floss (half the strands, as before) to sew two or three very small stitches to make an eye for each fish.

10 Pin the two notebook cover pieces together, lining up the edges as neatly as possible. Baste the two layers together with long stitches in black sewing thread, finishing the stitches loosely so they can be easily unpicked. Then remove the pins. Wrap the felt around the notebook, folding the ends inside the book covers to create flaps of equal size at the front and back. Use more long black stitches to baste each flap in place along the bottom edge only.

11 Position the pocket on the back of the cover, remove the cover from the book, and pin the pocket in place (only pinning through the two layers of the cover, not through the folded-over flap). Sew on the pocket with running stitch in turquoise sewing thread, sewing along the edges and then back again to create a continuous line of stitching. Hide the knot between the pocket and the cover, and start stitching at one bottom corner. Sew the first and last stitches of each row over the edges of the pocket.

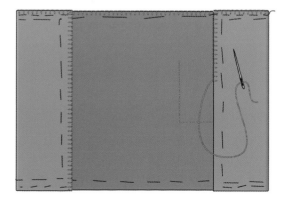

12 Put the book back inside the notebook cover, and baste the top of each flap in position with long stitches in black sewing thread. Use turquoise sewing thread to blanket stitch along the top and bottom of the notebook cover—sewing through four layers at each end to sew the flaps in place—and then down the edge of each flap. Finish the stitches neatly inside the notebook cover, then remove the black basting stitches.

angel teddy

This cute bear will be your guardian angel! It makes a special christening gift and can be personalized with an initial on the heart. It is not designed as a toy—if you're worried about keeping it out of little hands, add a loop of ribbon to the back and hang it on the wall. If you plan on this, you can leave the back of the halo and wings plain.

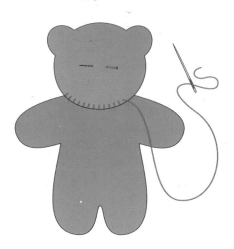

1 Use the templates to cut out two brown teddy bodies, one brown teddy face, two white wings, two orange halos, one pink heart, one light brown muzzle, two light brown ears, one dark brown nose, and two white eyes. Also cut two small black circles for the pupils (see page 8 for techniques for cutting out small shapes), and cut an extra wing and halo shape if you're using thin felt.

2 Pin the teddy face on top of one of the teddy body pieces. Sew it in place with straight stitches along the bottom of the face using brown sewing thread.

3 Sew the small pieces onto the face as pictured, using straight stitch in matching sewing threads and stitching through both layers of the teddy's face. First sew on the light brown ears and muzzle, then the dark brown nose, and finally the white eyes and black pupils.

4 Cut a length of dark brown embroidery floss and separate half the strands (so for six-stranded floss, use three strands). Switch to a larger needle if necessary and backstitch the teddy's smile, keeping the stitching inside the muzzle.

5 Pin the pink heart onto the teddy's chest. Cut a length of silver embroidery floss and separate half the strands: metallic embroidery floss is harder to work with than standard floss, so cut a shorter length than usual. Sew the heart in place with backstitch around the edge. If you want to personalize the heart, also add a stitched initial in the center.

6 Arrange gold sequins in circles on one of the halo shapes, covering it completely. Transfer the sequins one by one to the other halo shape, and sew them in place with a single strand of gold embroidery floss, using three stitches per sequin.

7 Fill in the gaps between the sequins with straight stitches in gold embroidery floss, using two strands of floss and leaving the edge of the halo clear. This piece will be the back of the halo. For the front you only need to decorate the top portion that will be visible above the bear's head—I used ten sequins, but this will vary depending on the size and position of the sequins.

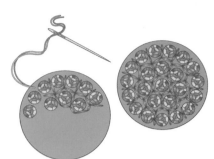

8 Pin the wing pieces together. Use half the strands of silver floss to sew the wings together using running stitch, sewing along and back again to create a continuous line of stitching. Turn the wings over and back again as you sew to keep the stitched line as straight as possible on both sides. Sew a line along the bottom of one wing, then sew scallops to look like overlapping feathers, and finish with a line along the top. Repeat this for the second wing. Finish the stitching in the center of the wings on the front—this will be hidden when the wings are sewn to the teddy. If you're just decorating the front of the wings, backstitch the design onto the front piece only, then sew the front and back together with whip stitch.

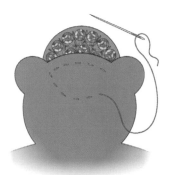

9 Sew the front of the halo to the back of the undecorated teddy's head, so the sequinned section is emerging from the top and the plain felt isn't visible. Use running stitch in brown sewing thread to sew along the bottom of the sequins and then around the bottom of the halo, sewing about ¼in (5mm) from the edge of the felt.

10 Turn the teddy over, and place the back of the halo on top of the front halo piece (adding a third layer of felt between them if required). Hold the halo together with your thumb and forefinger and use a single strand of gold embroidery floss to sew the pieces together with whip stitch around the edge.

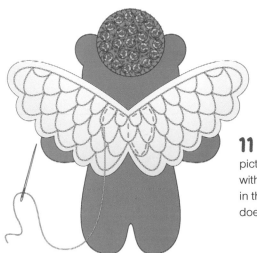

11 Position the wings on the back of the teddy, as pictured. Sew the center of the wings to the teddy with running stitch in white sewing thread, sewing in the gaps between the silver lines so the white doesn't overlap the silver.

12 Pin the front and back of the teddy together. Sew around the edge with whip stitch in brown sewing thread, leaving a gap for stuffing. Stuff the teddy lightly with polyester stuffing, using a pencil to poke the stuffing into all the corners. Then sew up the gap with more whip stitches and finish the stitching neatly on the back.

forget-me-not heart

A sweet pink heart—decorated with pretty blue forget-me-not flowers—which can be personalized with initials, a name, or a special date. It would make a great gift for Valentine's Day, or for a couple getting married or celebrating a special anniversary.

1 Use the templates to cut two large hearts from pink felt and about 25 forget-me-nots from blue felt. The flower shapes don't have to be perfect, but if you have problems cutting them you could enlarge the template slightly or buy die-cut felt flowers from a craft store.

2 Draw the initials, name, or date you want in pen on greaseproof paper or thin tracing paper. The simpler the letters, the easier they will be to embroider. Pin the paper to the center of one of the pink hearts.

3 Using a large needle and blue embroidery floss, sew along the pencil lines using small, even backstitches. Then carefully tear away the paper to remove it, using a pin to remove any little, fiddly pieces.

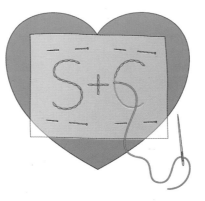

You will need:

Templates on page 117

Pink felt, approx. 6¾ × 11in (17 × 28cm)

Blue felt, approx. 4¾ × 6¾in (12 × 17cm)

Yellow seed beads, size 8/0

Blue and white stranded embroidery flosses (threads)

Pink and blue sewing threads

Narrow pink ribbon, approx. ¼in (5mm) wide, 8in (20cm) long

Polyester stuffing

Needles, scissors, pins

Pen

Greaseproof paper or thin tracing paper

4 Add the felt flowers to the heart to fill the space around the embroidery—you may find it helpful to arrange the flowers on the undecorated heart first to plan the layout. Sew the flowers in place with blue sewing thread, sewing a cross of two small stitches in the center of each flower.

5 Cut a length of white embroidery floss and separate two strands. Use these strands to sew ten stitches onto each flower, sewing one stitch between each petal and one slightly shorter stitch on each petal. Start the stitching away from the center of the flowers so the floss knot isn't in the center and won't keep getting caught by the needle.

6 Sew a yellow seed bead into the center of each flower using matching yellow sewing thread. Sew the bead flat like an "O" using three or four stitches.

7 Pin the decorated heart to the plain backing heart and trim any excess felt from the backing shape (the embroidery may have caused the heart shape to shrink slightly). Then remove the pins and set aside the decorated heart.

8 Fold the ribbon to make a loop and, with ⅜in (1cm) overlapping the felt, whip stitch the ribbon ends to the back of the backing heart using matching sewing thread.

9 Pin the front and back of the heart together so the ribbon ends are sandwiched between them. Sew the two hearts together with more pink sewing thread, sewing around the edge with whip stitch and leaving a gap to stuff the heart. Lightly stuff the heart with polyester stuffing then continue sewing along the edge to close the gap. Finish the stitches neatly on the back.

cat & mouse puppets

This set of fun toys has a cat hand puppet, three mice finger puppets, and a block of cheese! I made a stripy ginger cat, but you could adapt the colors and embroidered markings to match your own cat, or one in a favorite story.

The cat

1 Use the templates to cut two cat pieces and two tails from orange felt, two white eyes, two black pupils, one light orange tummy, two pink ears, and a pink nose.

2 Sew the eyes, pupils, ears, and nose to the face of one of the cat pieces using straight stitch and matching sewing threads. Then sew the tummy piece to the bottom of the cat with light orange sewing thread, using straight stitch around the curve and running stitch along the bottom edge.

3 Cut a length of black embroidery floss and separate half the strands (so for six-stranded floss, use three strands). Switch to a larger needle if necessary and backstitch the smile. Then cut a length of white embroidery floss, separate half the strands, and backstitch six white whiskers.

4 Cut a length of light orange embroidery floss and separate half the strands, as before. Use these strands to embroider stripes on the front of the cat and also on one of the tail pieces. Sew a series of backstitched lines at the top and sides of the cat, and along the edge of the tail, varying the lengths of the lines as pictured. Trim any loose threads.

5 Pin the two tail pieces together, and sew around the edges with whip stitch in orange sewing thread, leaving the bottom edge open. Remove the pins and stuff the tail very lightly with small pieces of polyester stuffing, using a pencil to poke the stuffing into the end of the tail. Then sew up the bottom edge with more whip stitches.

You will need:

Templates on page 117

Orange felt, approx. 10¼ × 12in (26 × 30cm)

Light orange felt, approx. 2¾ x 3in (7 × 8cm)

Yellow felt, approx. 3 × 6in (8 x 15cm)

White felt, approx. 3 × 5½in (8 x 14cm)

Brown felt, approx. 3 × 4½in (8 × 11cm)

Gray felt, approx. 3 × 4½in (8 × 11cm)

Pink felt, approx. 2¾ × 3in (7 x 8cm)

Small piece of black felt

Matching sewing threads

Light orange, black, and white stranded embroidery flosses (threads)

Narrow pink ribbon, approx. ¼in (5mm) wide, 2¾in (7cm) long for each mouse

Polyester stuffing

Pencil

Needles, scissors, pins

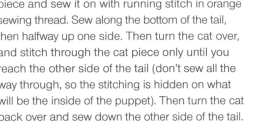

6 Position the tail in the center of the plain cat piece and sew it on with running stitch in orange sewing thread. Sew along the bottom of the tail, then halfway up one side. Then turn the cat over, and stitch through the cat piece only until you reach the other side of the tail (don't sew all the way through, so the stitching is hidden on what will be the inside of the puppet). Then turn the cat back over and sew down the other side of the tail.

7 Pin together the front and back of the cat and sew them using whip stitch in orange sewing thread. Start at one bottom corner and sew around until you reach the other bottom corner, leaving the bottom edge open. Remove the pins as you sew and finish the stitching neatly on the back.

The mice

1 For each mouse you want to make, use the templates to cut out two mouse pieces from white, brown, or gray felt, and two pink ears. Also cut out two small pink circles for the nose (see page 8 for techniques for cutting out small shapes).

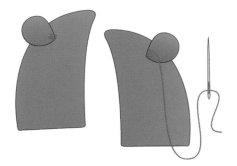

2 Position one ear on one of the mouse pieces, as pictured. Sew it in place with three or four stitches in pink sewing thread. Turn the second mouse piece over, and sew the second ear in place, so that when the front and back of the mouse are lined up the ears are in the same position.

3 Cut a length of black embroidery floss and separate half the strands, as before. Use these strands, and a larger needle if necessary, to sew an eye on to the mouse. Sew a very small star of four overlapping stitches and then sew over and over it to create a round eye. Repeat this for the other mouse piece, making sure the eye is in a similar position. Alternatively, you can cut two small black felt circles to use for the eyes and sew these in place with black sewing thread.

4 Sew the small pink circles to the tip of the mouse's nose. Use pink sewing thread and sew one circle to one mouse piece with a couple of small stitches in the center, then sew the second circle to the second mouse piece, so the two sides of the mouse are sewn together at the nose. Then whip stitch around the edges of the pink circles, sewing them together. Turn the mouse over and back again to ensure the stitches don't extend beyond the pink felt, then finish the stitching inside.

5 Cut a 2¾in (7cm) piece of narrow pink ribbon, trimming it at an angle to help prevent fraying. Fold the end of the ribbon in half lengthways and sew it together with small stitches in gray, white, or brown sewing thread (to match the mouse the tail is for). Then sew the ribbon in place with whip stitches to the back edge of one mouse piece, so the sewn end will be hidden inside the puppet. You can just sew the ribbon flat without folding it first, but folding it makes the ribbon curl nicely.

6 Pin or hold the two sides of the mouse together and whip stitch around the edge with matching sewing thread, leaving the bottom edge open. Repeat all the steps to make a trio of mice in different colors.

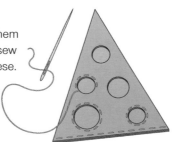

The cheese

1 Cut three yellow cheese shapes using the template. Cut a series of circular holes in one layer at random. To do this, fold the felt over and cut out a semicircle, which when unfolded becomes a roughly circular hole, then trim it to make the circle more even. You may want to practice this on some scrap pieces of felt before you begin, and remember to cut slightly smaller holes than you need to allow for trimming.

2 Place the cheese with holes in on one of the other cheese pieces. Hold or pin the layers together and sew them with yellow sewing thread. Use small running stitches to sew around each hole and along the bottom edge of the cheese.

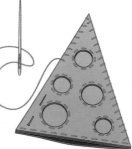

3 Pin all three layers together and use more yellow sewing thread to whip stitch them together, leaving the bottom edge open.

Chapter 3
Homewares

owl egg cozy

A loveable owl peering up at you will make every breakfast more fun. I used eco felt to make my owl, but any washable craft felt is suitable, as long as it's thick enough to support the embroidered details. Not a fan of boiled eggs? Follow all the steps shown and when your owl is finished, fill it with lavender then sew along the bottom to make a scented sachet.

1 Using the templates provided cut out two brown body shapes, four ginger wing shapes, two light brown eye shapes, and one dark brown beak. Cut out two small circles from the dark brown felt for the pupils (see page 8 for tips on cutting out small shapes).

2 Position the wings on the body shapes as pictured and pin them in place. On one of the body shapes, arrange the eyes, pupils, and beak to create the owl's face. Sew the pupils to the eyes and sew the beak in place with straight stitches and dark brown thread. Next, sew on the eyes with straight stitches and light brown thread.

You will need:

Templates on page 118

Brown felt, approx.
4 × 8¾in (10 × 22cm)

Ginger felt, approx.
2½ × 5in (6 × 13cm)

Small pieces of dark brown
and very light brown felt

Matching sewing threads

Peach and dusky pink stranded
embroidery flosses (threads)

Needles, scissors, pins

3 Cut lengths of peach and dusky pink embroidery floss and separate half the strands (so for six-stranded floss, use three strands). Switch to a larger needle if necessary. With peach floss, sew a line of running stitch down the curved inner edge of all four wings and remove the pins. With dusky pink floss, sew long straight stitches radiating out from the pupils; make them long enough to slightly overlap the edge of the eyes and finish on the brown body.

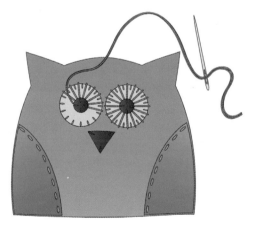

4 Sew several lines of zigzag stitches across the front of the owl, alternating the rows between peach and pink embroidery floss.

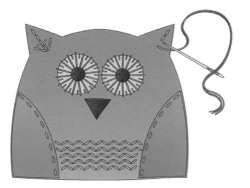

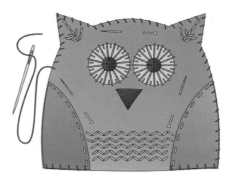

5 Using peach embroidery floss, backstitch lines on the owl's ear tufts to decorate them. Sew a line down the center of each ear, with four diagonal lines coming from it—like an arrow with two points.

6 Sew the bottom edge of each wing to the body with whip stitch and brown thread. Wrong sides facing, pin the front and back of the owl together and use more brown thread to whip stitch around the edge, leaving the bottom open. Remove the pins and secure the thread inside the owl.

little house doorstop

Inspired by fairytale cottages, you can use this house as a cute decoration, or add parcels of dried beans to weight it for use as a doorstop. Always hold the doorstop at the base when carrying it to avoid stretching the felt with the weight of the beans, and don't use it in a bathroom or other very humid room.

You will need:

Templates on page 118
Light blue felt, approx.
14½ × 25¼in (36 × 64cm)
Bright red felt, approx.
12 × 16½in (30 × 42cm)
White felt, approx.
5½ × 5½in (14 × 14cm)
Matching sewing threads
Black stranded embroidery
floss (thread)
Polyester toy stuffing
Dried beans or lentils,
approx. 2lb (1kg)
Four small plastic food bags
Parcel tape
Needles, scissors, pins

1 Use the templates to cut two front/back pieces from light blue felt. Cut two blue pieces measuring 6 x 6¾in (15 x 17cm) for the sides and one 6 x 6in (15 x 15cm) for the base. From red felt and using the templates, cut two front/back roof edges, two side roof edges, and one door. Cut two red pieces measuring 4¼ x 6in (11 x 15cm) for side roofs and six 1 x 2¼in (2.5 x 5.5cm) for shutters. Cut out one door window from white felt using the template and three squares 2½ x 2½in (6 x 6cm) for windows.

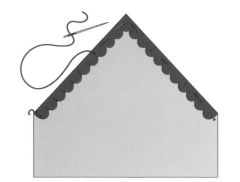

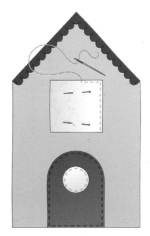

2 Pin one roof edge piece to the top of each wall of the house. Sew the edge pieces in place with red sewing thread, sewing one straight stitch between each scallop and removing the pins as you sew.

3 Arrange the door and windows on the walls and pin them in position. Each side wall should have one window and the front wall should have one window, a door, and a round window in the top of the door. Use neat running stitch in matching sewing thread to sew all these pieces in place.

4 Cut a length of black embroidery floss and set aside less than half of the strands (I set aside two of the six strands in my embroidery floss). Using the remaining strands and a large needle, sew a small star shape (made with four overlapped stitches) as a doorknob, and backstitch frames on the three large wall windows and the small window in the door. Sew around the edge of each white window shape and then across it twice to form a cross within the square or circle.

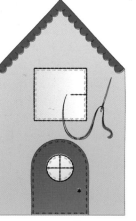

5 Fold one of the red shutter pieces in half lengthways and hold it between your thumb and forefinger. Make a curved cut in the felt near the top so that when you open the shutter piece out again it has a cut-out heart shape (I recommend practicing this on some scrap felt first). Repeat this for all the shutters.

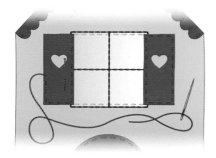

6 Pin one shutter to each side of the windows, so they slightly overlap the embroidered window frames. Sew them in place with running stitch in red sewing thread, then remove the pins.

7 Sew the pieces of the house together using whip stitch to join the edges. Sew the two roof pieces together with matching red thread along one long edge, and sew the top of each wall piece to the roof with more red thread. Then use blue thread to sew the walls together.

8 Fill two plastic food bags with dried beans or lentils, adding 1lb (500g) to each. Seal the bags with parcel tape, removing as much air as possible, then place each one inside a second bag and seal them again. These will be the doorstop weights.

9 Lightly stuff the house with polyester stuffing, add the parcels of lentils/beans at the bottom and fill the space around them with more stuffing. Use whip stitch to sew the base piece on to the bottom of the house, starting with red thread to sew along the bottom of the door, then switching to blue thread. Add any extra stuffing (if needed) as you sew and finish the stitching neatly on the bottom.

flower napkin rings

This set of floral napkin rings would be a great addition to your tableware—make them in your favorite colors or to match plates. They'd also make a great hostess gift. I used 100 percent wool felt, but any craft felt is suitable, though you may need to use an extra layer to make the rings sturdy enough to keep their shape.

1 For each napkin ring you make, cut two 5½ x 1¼in (14 x 3cm) pieces of green felt for the rings. Use the templates to cut one lighter green leaf and the four pieces to make the flower from your choice of colors. I used two shades of the same color for my flowers, cutting the small circle and small flower pieces from the darker shade, and the large circle and large flower pieces from the lighter shade.

2 Place one ring piece on top of the other and line them up neatly. Pin them together at one end, and curve them into a ring shape. Trim any excess felt from the inner ring and remove the pin.

3 Fold the two pieces into a loop (shorter piece on the inside), holding the ends together. Start stitching so the knot is hidden between the layers, and whip stitch all four edges together with green sewing thread. Pull the loop out to form a circle, pressing the sewn edge flat.

4 Sew around the long edges of the ring with running stitch in green thread, taking care not to sew too tightly and pucker the felt. Hide the knot between the layers, as before, and finish the stitching at the seam on the outside of the ring (where it will be hidden when you add the leaf and flower).

5 Cut a length of embroidery floss to match the color of the large flower and large circle pieces. Separate half the strands (so for six-stranded floss, use three strands), and use them to embroider the flower, switching to a larger needle if necessary. Layer all four flower pieces as pictured, and sew them together with a star shape of eight stitches in the center. Then sew three long stitches onto each petal, sewing through both layers of the petal and making the middle stitch slightly longer than the other two.

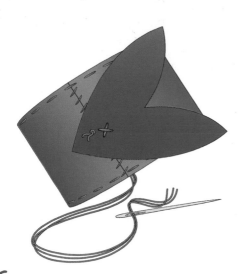

6 Using more embroidery floss, sew the leaf piece in place on top of the ring seam, so the narrow end of the leaf slightly overlaps the seam. Sew the leaf in place with a cross of two small stitches, starting the stitching from the top so the knot will be hidden in the next step. Do not fasten off the floss.

7 Place the flower on top of the leaf as pictured, and use the floss to sew it in position with a line of small running stitches around the edge of the smaller circle. Sew around the circle and then back again to create a continuous line of stitching, sewing through all the layers to attach the flower to the napkin ring. Finish the stitching neatly inside the ring. Repeat Steps 2–7 for each napkin ring.

squirrel & oak coasters

A pair of woodland coasters decorated with an oak leaf, acorns, and a squirrel. I grew up with gray squirrels in our back yard, but you might prefer to sew red squirrels on your coasters, and you can sew on green or brown oak leaves. Wool felt, or other thicker or stiffer felt, is perfect for this project as it will help the coasters keep their shape as you sew.

1 Use the templates to cut out a green or light brown oak leaf, a gray or red squirrel, two light brown large acorn caps, and two large and one small ginger acorns. Also cut out two coaster shapes from one shade of green felt and two more from another shade of green. Choose a color for the top of the coasters that the squirrel and oak leaf colors will stand out against (for example, a light green oak leaf needs a darker green background). If for the bottom of the coasters you use felt that matches the embroidery floss edging (see Step 6), it will be easier to finish the stitching neatly as the stitches will be less visible.

You will need:

Templates on page 119

Gray or red felt, approx.
3 x 3½in (8 × 9cm)
for two coasters

Green or light brown felt,
approx. 2¾ × 3½in (7 × 9cm)
for two coasters

Small pieces of light brown,
ginger, black, and white felt

Matching sewing threads

Two shades of green felt,
approx. 4¾ × 9½in (12 × 24cm)
per color for two coasters

Green stranded embroidery
floss (thread)

Needles, scissors, pins

2 Arrange the small pieces as pictured on the two circles that will be the top of the coasters. Baste them in position with long stitches in black sewing thread, finishing the stitching loosely so you can easily unpick it later. Sew all the pieces in place with straight stitches around the edges, using matching sewing threads. Then remove the black stitches.

3 Using doubled green or brown sewing thread, backstitch veins on the oak leaf. Sew slightly curved lines, one down the center of the leaf and one branching out from the central line to each leaf point. If you want the veins of the leaf to really stand out, use a slightly darker shade of thread.

4 With a double thickness of gray sewing thread, add details to the squirrel. Use the dotted lines on the pattern piece as a guide and backstitch curved lines to "draw" the leg and the tail. Also sew two small stitches on the ear in an upside-down "V" shape.

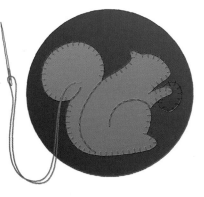

5 Cut out a small white circle for the eye and a very small black circle for the pupil (see page 8 for techniques for cutting out small shapes). You could instead use black stitches to form the pupil, but don't use a bead as the coaster should be completely flat. Use black sewing thread to backstitch a curved line for the smile, and to sew the pupil in place on the white eye. Then use white sewing thread to sew around the eye with straight stitches.

6 Pin the fronts and backs of the coasters together. Cut a length of green embroidery floss to contrast with the top of the coasters, separate half the strands (so for six-stranded floss, use three strands), and switch to a larger needle if necessary. Use the embroidery floss to sew the front and back of each coaster together with blanket stitch, removing the pins as you sew. Hide the knots between the two layers and finish the stitching very neatly on the back.

teatime tea cozy An appliquéd tea cozy inspired by girly tea parties! The cozy is decorated with a retro cake stand covered in yummy cakes, and is big enough to fit most large family teapots. It takes a while to sew on all the pieces that make up the appliquéd picture but if you love tea (and cake), this is the project for you.

1 Using the templates, cut out two cozy shapes from white felt and two from turquoise felt. Then cut out the two cake stand plates and the round handle from turquoise felt, and cut two cake stand uprights from gray felt. Note that the cozy and cake plate templates are for half the shape, so fold the felt in half and pin the template on with the dotted line on the fold to cut out the whole shape.

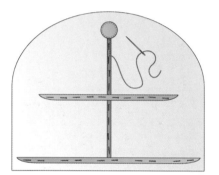

2 Position all the cake stand pieces on one of the white cozy pieces, as pictured. Use a ruler to help get the cake stand as straight as possible: the top of the handle should be ⅝in (1.5cm) from the top edge of the cozy, and there should be a 4in (10cm) gap between the two turquoise plates. Pin all the pieces in place and sew them on with straight stitch in matching thread, removing the pins as you sew.

3 The cake stand is filled with four types of cake—large cupcakes, small cupcakes, Battenberg, and Swiss roll. Following the instructions, cut out all the pieces you need for each cake, arrange them on the cozy, and pin them in place. Sew them all according to the instructions, removing the pins as you sew.

The large cupcake

Cut three pieces for each large cupcake using the templates: a light brown cupcake, large pastel frosting, and a large patterned felt cupcake case. Trim the top of the case with pinking shears. Place the cupcake in position, then arrange the case and frosting pieces on top so there's a small bit of cupcake still visible between them. Pin the pieces in place and sew around all the edges with straight stitch and matching threads, sewing one stitch in each V of the pinked edge along the top of the cupcake case.

Top the cake with a red cherry. Cut a cherry from red felt using the template and sew it on the top of the cupcake with a small cross of two stitches at the top of the cherry and red straight stitches around the edge.

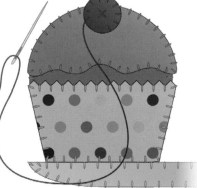

You will need:

Templates on page 120

White felt, approx. 15 × 24in (37 × 60cm)

Turquoise felt, approx. 15 × 26¼in (37 × 67cm)

Gray felt, approx. 1¼ × 4½in (3 × 11cm)

Yellow felt, approx. 3 × 3in (8 × 8cm)

Pink felt, approx. 3 × 3in (8 × 8cm)

Light brown felt, approx. 2¾ × 8¼in (7 × 21cm)

Cream felt, approx. 6¼ × 6¼in (16 × 16cm)

Raspberry pink felt, approx. 3 × 3½in (8 × 9cm)

Assorted shades of pastel felt, approx. 2 × 2¾in (5 × 7cm) in each color

Small piece of red felt

Pieces of patterned felt, approx. 3 × 8¼in (8 × 21cm) in total

Matching sewing threads for all colors

Assorted seed beads and bugle beads

Polyester batting

Turquoise stranded embroidery floss

Needles, scissors, pins

Long pins

Pinking shears

Ruler

The small cupcake

Cut two pieces for each small cupcake: small pastel frosting and a small cupcake case from patterned felt. Position the frosting so it overlaps the cupcake case so the top edge of the case can't be seen. Pin the pieces in place and sew them on with straight stitches in matching threads. Decorate the frosting with beaded "sprinkles." Using doubled thread to match the frosting, sew on seed or bugle beads at random, as if they've been sprinkled on top.

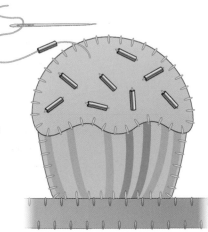

The Battenberg

Use the templates to cut out one Battenberg shape from cream felt, two pink felt squares, and two yellow felt squares for each cake. Sew all the pieces in place with straight stitches in matching thread. Pin and sew the cream Battenberg shape first, then add the squares inside. Line up all four squares so their edges meet neatly, sew small stitches at each corner to hold them in place, and then continue to sew around all the edges.

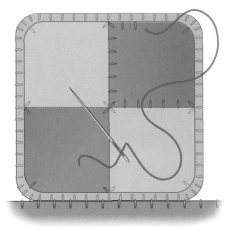

The Swiss roll

Use the Swiss roll template provided to cut out one cream or light brown cake shape, and one raspberry-pink shape. Carefully cut out a spiral shape from the raspberry piece, starting at the outside and working inward. Sew the cream shape in place with straight stitches in matching cream thread. Then, arrange the raspberry spiral on top and sew it in position with running stitches down the center in matching thread. Cutting out the spiral can be a bit fiddly, so if you prefer you can embroider a spiral with raspberry embroidery floss, backstitching to create a continuous line.

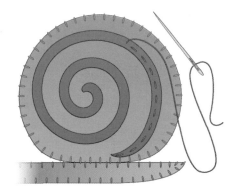

4 Using the cozy template, cut out two cozy shapes from polyester batting. Trim off a small amount all around the edge so you end up with two shapes slightly smaller than the felt cozy pieces.

5 Place one piece of batting in the center of one of the turquoise cozy shapes, and place the decorated cozy front on top to create a sandwich of three layers. Pin the layers together with long pins.

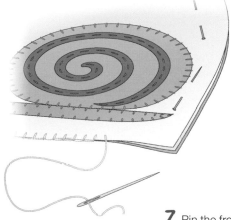

6 With white thread, first stitch along the bottom of the cozy, sewing the layers together with blanket stitch. Then sew a line of running stitch around the curved edge of the cozy. Finish all the stitches on the turquoise side as this will be the inside of the cozy. Remove the pins and repeat with the remaining pieces to make the back.

7 Pin the front and back of the cozy together with long pins, taking care to line up all the edges accurately. Cut a length of turquoise embroidery floss and separate half the strands (so for six-stranded floss, use three strands). Switching to a larger needle if necessary, sew the front and back of the cozy together along the curve using evenly spaced blanket stitches. Remove the pins as you sew and finish the stitches neatly inside the cozy.

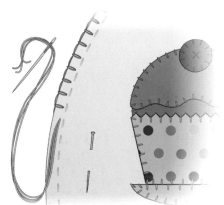

toadstool hot water bottle cover

Keep your hot water bottle warm for hours and hours with this appliquéd cover. I used thick, needle-felted felt sheets for the cover, but if you can't find those, recycled sweater felt is perfect for this project. I made the toadstools from 100 percent wool felt, but any craft felt will do. You could also use a selection of white buttons for the spots on the toadstools instead of cutting out all those circles! The pattern fits a standard hot water bottle.

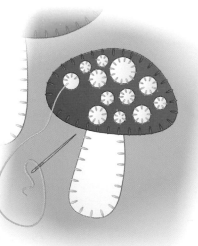

You will need:

Templates on page 121

Very thick felt, approx.
16½ × 20½in (42 × 52cm)

Red felt, approx. 5½ × 8¼in
(14 × 21cm)

White felt, approx. 6¾ × 8¼in
(17 × 21cm)

Red and white sewing threads

Red stranded embroidery
floss (thread)

Needles, scissors, pins

Long pins

1 Use the templates to cut the front and two back pieces of the cover from very thick felt. For the top back, cut from the dashed line up around the top edge of the template and down to the dashed line, then cut across this line. For the lower back, cut from the dotted line down around the bottom edge of the template and up to the dotted line, then cut across this line. Pin the templates in place with long pins and cut the pieces out carefully. If you're using a recycled sweater, make sure you cut all the pieces with the "right" (outer) side of the sweater facing toward you.

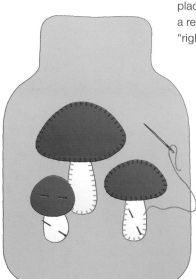

2 Cut out the three toadstool caps from red felt and the three toadstool stalks from white felt. Arrange the shapes on the front cover piece and pin them in position.

3 With matching red and white sewing threads, sew all the toadstool pieces in place with straight stitch. Where one toadstool overlaps another, sew the one behind first and made sure the caps and stems are butted up as close as possible to each other.

4 Cut out lots of small circles from white felt, in an assortment of sizes (see page 8 for tips on cutting out small circles). Arrange the circles on the paper toadstool cap templates at random and when you're happy with the arrangement, transfer the circles one by one to the same positions on the felt caps to sew them in place. Sew on the circles with straight stitches in white thread and finish the stitching on the back.

5 Turn the decorated front piece over and position both envelope pieces on top of it so the top piece slightly overlaps the bottom and all the "right" sides of the felt are facing outward. Pin the pieces together with long pins.

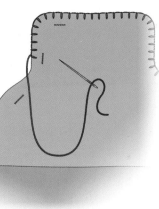

6 Thread a large needle with red embroidery floss and sew around the edge with blanket stitch. Start at the envelope opening and stitch all the way around the outside of the cover, removing the pins as you sew. Start and finish the stitches inside where the knots and workings won't be visible.

butterfly cushion

A giant pink and purple butterfly covered in lots of sparkly sequins—perfect for a little girl's room. I made my butterfly take up the whole cushion front, but a smaller butterfly on a lilac cushion would look great. Make sure you have lots of purple thread before starting this project, you don't want to run out halfway through!

You will need:

Templates on page 122

Lilac felt, approx. 17 × 37in (43 × 93cm)

Purple felt, approx. 16½ × 16½in (42 × 42cm)

Purple and black sewing threads

Purple stranded embroidery floss (thread)

Four shades of pink and purple felt, approx. 16½ × 14in (42 × 35cm) for the largest layer, approx. 6¾ × 8¾in (17 × 22cm) for the smallest layer

Lots of pink and purple sequins

Needles, scissors, pins

Long pins

Cushion pad, 16 × 16in (40 × 40cm)

Tape measure, ruler, paper, adhesive tape, felt-tip pen

1 Measure your cushion pad and add an extra ¼in (5mm) on each edge for the front of your cushion cover—my pad is 16 x 16in (40 x 40cm), so my cover is 16½ x 16½in (42 x 42cm). The back is an envelope closure of two pieces. One is 16½ x 8¼in (42 x 21cm), and the second is 16½ x 11¼in (42 x 28.5cm.) You can make paper patterns or draw the pieces directly onto the back of the lilac felt. Cut out the three pieces.

2 Use the templates to cut out other pieces for your cushion (resize the templates on a photocopier as required). Cut two body pieces, two antennae, and two each of wing top 1 and wing bottom 1, all from purple felt. Cut the remaining pieces from an assortment of pink and purple felt, cutting two of each shape and cutting pieces with the same number from the same color felt: also, cut pieces 5 and 6 from the same color. The templates are for the left wing; flip them over for the right wing.

3 Position all the butterfly pieces—except the small antenna pieces—on the front cushion piece. Place the two body pieces on top of each other in the center of the cushion and then arrange the wing pieces either side of the body. Layer the pieces from 1–5 from bottom to top, with the teardrop-shaped number 6 pieces at the base of the wings as pictured. Pin all the pieces in place and then baste them in position with long stitches of black sewing thread. Finish the stitches loosely so they can easily be removed later, then remove all the pins.

4 Sew around the edges of all the pieces with straight stitches in purple sewing thread. Start by sewing the butterfly body, then sew the inside edges of the wings as flush as possible to it. Then gradually sew all the layers of the wings in place, removing the long black stitches as you finish each wing section.

5 Stitch two slightly curved lines from the top of the butterfly body. Use purple floss and a large needle to sew running stitch, then sew back again to create a continuous line. Be careful not to pull the stitches too tight and pucker the felt. Sew the two antenna pieces to the ends of the lines with straight stitch in purple sewing thread.

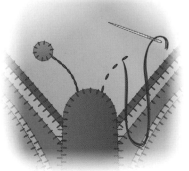

6 Arrange lots of pink and purple sequins on the wings, plus one on each of the antennae. Copy the arrangement pictured or create your own pattern, but make sure that each wing is the mirror image of the other. Draw a sketch or take a digital photo to use as a reference. Remove the sequins and then sew them in position one by one. Use purple sewing thread, sewing each sequin in place with three stitches.

7 Turn the decorated front cushion piece face down and lay both envelope pieces on top of it, with the smaller piece overlapping the larger one. Pin the pieces together with long pins.

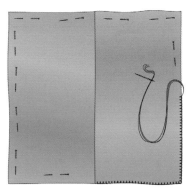

8 Cut a length of purple embroidery floss and separate half the strands (so for six-stranded floss, use three strands). Using these strands, and a larger needle if necessary, sew around the edge of the cushion with blanket stitch. Start at the envelope opening and stitch all the way around the outside, removing the pins as you sew. Start and finish the stitches inside the cover. When the cover is finished, squish the cushion pad through the envelope opening and plump it up.

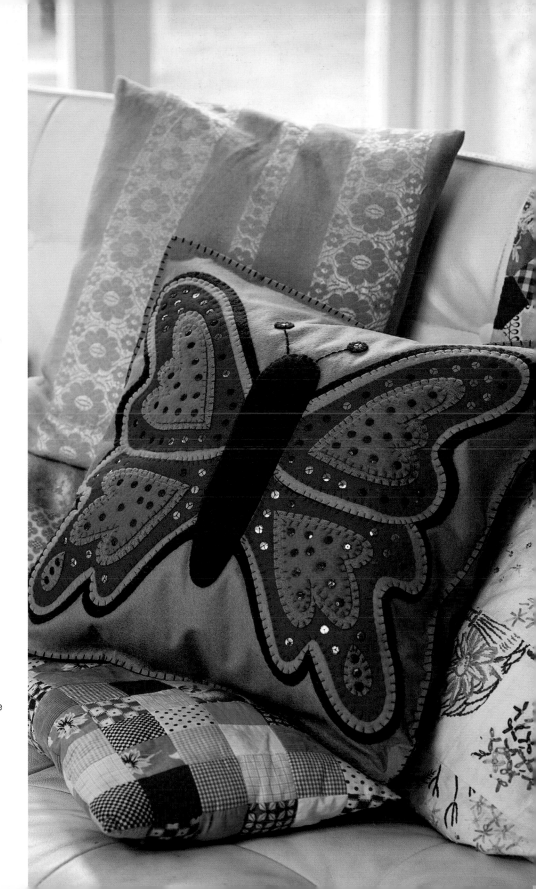

lovebirds mobile

An embroidered mobile made with birds, hearts, and felt balls in mix-and-match colors. I chose pinks, purples, and blues, but this design can be easily adapted to suit any color scheme. The pieces take a while to sew, but you can save time by making a smaller mobile, or just a single strand. Make sure you hang your mobile well out of reach of babies and small children, and out of direct sunlight to avoid the colors fading.

1 For each color you want, use the templates to cut out two bird shapes, two wing shapes, two large hearts, two medium hearts, two small hearts, and two eyes.

2 Plan the arrangement of your mobile. The birds and hearts use pairs of contrasting colors. Each bird is two bird shapes (color A), two wings (color A), two eyes (color B), and two small hearts (color B) on the wings. Each heart is two large hearts (color C), and two medium hearts (color D.) Make a sketch or take a digital photograph for reference.

You will need:

Templates on page 123

Felt in eight assorted colors, approx. 8¼ × 8in (21 × 20cm) in each color

Matching sewing threads and stranded embroidery flosses (threads)

Felt balls in coordinating colors, approx. 20

Narrow ribbon in a coordinating color, 4yds (4m)

Large wooden embroidery hoop, 8in (20cm) diameter

Needles, scissors, pins

Large needle

3 Use embroidery floss to sew each of the pieces together. Set aside half the strands (so for six-stranded floss, use three strands). To sew the birds, pin a wing (color A) to the matching bird and sew it on with running stitches in contrasting floss (color B). Then sew a small heart (color B) onto the center of the wing with a cross of two stitches. Next, switch embroidery floss (to color A) and sew the eye (color B) in position with a star of four stitches. Repeat for the other side of the bird.

4 To sew the hearts, pin a medium heart (color D) in the center of a large heart (color C). Sew it in place with running stitches around the edge and a star of four large stitches in the center (using embroidery floss color C). Repeat for the other side of the heart.

5 Using your sketch or photo, lay out your mobile pieces. Add felt balls as spacers between the shapes, using any arrangement you like but always with a ball at the bottom of each strand.

6 Cut about 1yd (1m) of ribbon for each strand, knot it at one end and thread a large needle with the other end. Thread the ribbon through the bottom felt ball, and trim off any excess below the knot. Add the pieces to the ribbon in sequence, pinning one half of each bird and heart to the ribbon and threading the balls onto it using the needle. Make sure the pieces are evenly spaced and leave at least 12in (30cm) of ribbon free at the top of each strand for making up the mobile.

7 Carefully whip stitch the ribbon to the back of the bird and heart halves where there is a double layer of felt (where the wing is sewn on the bird and where the middle heart is sewn on the large heart). Only sew through one layer of the felt, taking care that the stitches don't show on the right side. If you're making individual mobile strands, fold the ribbon over when you reach the top and sew it in place to form a loop. Remove the pins.

8 Pin the matching halves of the birds and hearts together. Sew them together with running stitch around the edge, using matching sewing thread. Finish the stitches neatly as they will be visible.

9 Tie each strand in place on the inner ring of a wooden embroidery hoop (the outer ring of the hoop is not needed). Knot the ribbon securely, leaving at least 10in (25cm) free above the ring. Use a large needle to thread all four strands of the mobile through a felt ball, one at a time, and pull the ribbon through until the ball is in the center of the hoop and the mobile is hanging evenly. Knot the ribbons together above the ball and use them to hang the mobile.

lion coffee cozy This happy lion will help keep your coffee nice and warm! The cozy is designed to fit a standard 8-cup cafetière or French press. It's a good idea to use washable felt for this project so that you can hand wash it in the event of any spills.

1 Use the templates to cut out all the pieces. Cut a face and body from light brown felt, a mane and tail from ginger felt, a moon and two eyes from white felt, a nose from black felt, three cozy pieces from royal blue felt, and a grass strip from very light brown or cream felt (the grass strip is the area below the dotted line across the cozy template). Also cut out two small black circles for pupils (see page 8 for techniques for cutting out small shapes).

2 Arrange the face and mane on the lion's body, and pin the layers together. Sew around the face with straight stitches in light brown sewing thread, sewing through all three layers. Remove the pins.

3 Sew a curved line inside each ear with backstitch in ginger sewing thread. Position the eyes, pupils, and nose on the face and sew the pupils and nose in place with straight stitches in black sewing thread. Use more black sewing thread to sew the whiskers, sewing one single long stitch for each whisker. Then use doubled black sewing thread to backstitch the mouth. Finally, use white thread to straight stitch around the eyes.

4 Cut a series of narrow triangles out of one side of the grass strip. Pin the grass in place along the bottom of one cozy piece and straight stitch it in position with matching sewing thread, sewing stitches completely over the very narrow tips of the grass and leaving the straight bottom edge unstitched. This step is quite time consuming, so as an alternative you could cut a wobbly line along one long edge of the grass strip to represent earth instead of long grass.

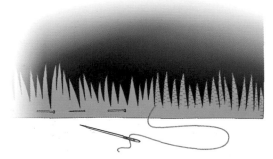

You will need:

Templates on page 123

Royal blue felt, approx. 12 × 19in (30 × 48cm)

Light brown felt, approx. 7 × 7½in (18 x 19cm)

Ginger felt, approx. 4¾ × 5in (12 × 13cm)

Pale brown or cream felt, approx. 2 × 12in (5 × 30cm)

Small pieces of black and white felt

Matching sewing threads

Light brown stranded embroidery floss (thread)

Lots of gold star sequins, approx. ¼in (5mm) diameter

Three large buttons

Narrow blue ribbon, approx. 24in (60cm)

Needles, scissors, pins

5 Trim any light brown felt showing behind the spikes of the ginger mane. Pin the lion on the cozy piece as pictured, placing it off-center so that there is plenty of room on the right for the tail and a row of buttons.

6 Sew around the mane with straight stitches in ginger sewing thread, then around the body with light brown thread. Use ginger thread to backstitch a line to divide the back legs (the dotted line on the template is a guide). Sew three small stitches on each paw, evenly spaced on the front paws and clustered toward the left on the back paws.

7 Cut a length of light brown embroidery floss and separate half the strands (so for six-stranded floss, use three strands). Backstitch curved lines on the mane, one line radiating out from the lion's head to each spike.

8 Use light brown embroidery floss to backstitch the tail as pictured. Place the ginger tail piece on the end and straight stitch it in place with ginger sewing thread.

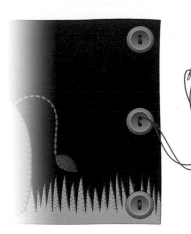

9 Sew a row of three buttons along the right-hand edge of the cozy. Use doubled blue sewing thread to sew them securely in place.

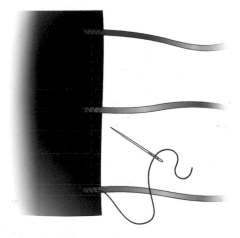

10 Cut three 8in (20cm) lengths of narrow blue ribbon, cutting the ends at an angle to help prevent fraying. Sew the ribbons to one of the undecorated cozy pieces, at the opposite end to the buttons but with the same spacing. With ⅜in (1cm) overlapping the felt, whip stitch the ribbon ends in place using blue sewing thread. Sew a line of running stitches between the ribbons so you don't have to keep finishing and restarting the stitching.

11 Position the moon on the cozy as pictured and sew it in place with straight stitch in white sewing thread. Then sew lots of small gold star sequins at random across the top part of the cozy. Sew the sequins in place with light brown sewing thread and three stitches per sequin.

12 Pin the three cozy pieces together, so the piece with the ribbon ends is sandwiched in the middle. Sew the three layers together around the edge with matching sewing thread and neat blanket stitch, sewing a couple of extra stitches as you sew over where each ribbon sticks out. Remove the pins as you sew and finish the stitches on the back. To fasten the cozy, wind each ribbon twice around the corresponding button. Narrower cafètieres will need less ribbon, so trim any excess if necessary.

Chapter 4
Celebrations

peacock mask

Peacocks definitely know how to show off, and this vibrant peacock mask is the perfect accessory for New Year's Eve, Halloween, carnival, or any other costume party. The mask is decorated with a row of felt peacock feathers and lots of sparkle with gold sequins and gold embroidery floss details. If you prefer, you can sew a loop of elastic to the mask instead of the ribbon ties.

1 Use the templates to cut out two mask pieces from turquoise felt. To make sure the mask doesn't flop, use 100 percent wool felt, or thicker craft felt, or cut three pieces from thinner felt. Also cut out enough pieces to make five peacock feathers. Each peacock feather is made up of five layers of felt: navy-blue (piece 1), turquoise (piece 2), bronze or ginger (piece 3), bright spring-green (piece 4), and dark green (piece 5).

2 Layer the five pieces of one feather on top of each other and hold them together in the center with your thumb and forefinger. Sew around the edge of the central navy-blue shape with running stitch in navy thread, sewing through all the layers to hold them together. Then stitch around the edge of the turquoise shape with running stitch in turquoise thread.

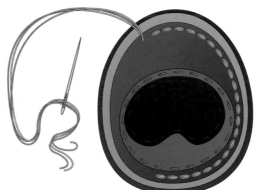

3 Cut a length of gold embroidery floss and separate half the strands (so for six-stranded floss, use three strands). Metallic floss is harder to work with than normal embroidery floss, so cut short lengths to avoid tangling. You may also need to switch to a larger needle. Carefully backstitch around the edge of the bronze feather shape.

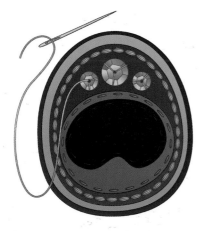

4 Using a single strand of the gold floss and three stitches per sequin, sew three gold sequins (one large and two small) to the top of the peacock feather, as pictured. Repeat Steps 2–4 to make up the other four peacock feathers.

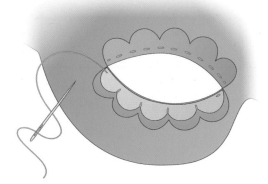

5 Cut out eight eye feather pieces using the templates. Cut two cream feathers (feather A = top, B = bottom) and two turquoise feathers (C = top, D = bottom) for each eye. The templates provided are for the left eye; flip the pieces over to use them for the right eye. Use matching sewing threads to sew the eye feathers in place on one mask piece. First sew on the turquoise pieces with a line of running stitch and then add the cream pieces on top and secure them with a single stitch between each feather and a stitch at each end.

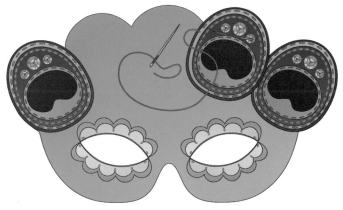

6 Sew the layered peacock feathers to the top of the mask, starting with the outer feathers and working inward. Use matching green sewing thread to sew around the green layer of each feather in running stitch. The feathers will overlap slightly. When you have sewn all five feathers in place, trim any turquoise felt from the mask piece that is visible behind the feathers along the top of the mask.

7 Decorate the mask with gold sequins, as in the main photograph. Sew five sequins (one large and four small) in a V shape in the center, and three sequins (one large and two small) in a line next to each eye. Use single strands of gold embroidery floss to sew the sequins in place, with three stitches per sequin.

8 Cut two lengths of turquoise ribbon, each about 20in (50cm) long. Sew one to each side of the undecorated mask piece (this will be the back of the mask), just below the row of peacock feathers. With the ends overlapping the felt by ¾in (2cm), sew the ribbons in place with whip stitches in matching turquoise thread. Trim the ends of the ribbons at an angle to help prevent fraying.

9 Pin the front and back mask pieces together, so the ribbon ends are sandwiched between them. Sew around the opening for each eye with cream sewing thread, using whip stitch to sew all the layers together. Hide the knots and finish the stitching between the layers.

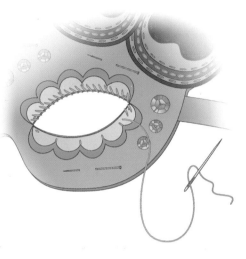

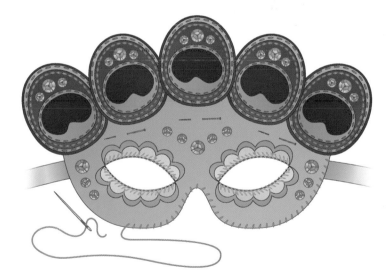

10 Trim any turquoise felt from the back mask piece that is showing behind the row of peacock feathers. Whip stitch around the bottom edge of the mask with turquoise thread, sewing the front and back together. Then sew around the top edge of the mask (around the row of peacock feathers) with whip stitch in dark green thread.

11 Cut out two beak pieces from cream felt using the template provided. Using cream sewing thread, sew the two pieces together using whip stitch. Hide the knot in between the two layers and finish the stitching neatly.

12 Turn the peacock mask over and sew the beak in place from the back, curving it to fit the curve of the mask. Use a length of cream thread to sew small whip stitches, starting in the center and sewing outward and then back to the center again in one direction and then the other so the beak is securely stitched in place. Finish the stitches neatly on the underside of the beak.

easter wreath

A wreath to hang in your home at Easter. This wreath would also look great in bright colors on a spring-green background, and you could decorate the eggs with sequins or tiny buttons instead of the embroidered patterns. If you don't want to make a whole wreath, individual embroidered eggs make lovely ornaments: just add backing felt to each egg and a loop of ribbon.

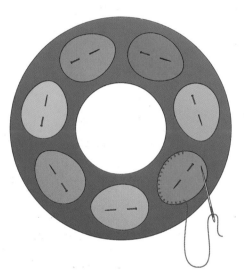

1 Use the templates to cut out two blue wreath shapes and seven pastel egg shapes, each one from a different color felt. Space the eggs out evenly around one of the wreath shapes, with a gap of approximately ⅜in (1cm) between each egg. Pin the eggs in position.

2 Sew all the eggs in place with straight stitch around the edges using matching sewing threads, then remove the pins.

You will need:

Templates on page 125

Blue felt, approx. 10 × 20in (25 × 50cm)

Seven pastel felt colors, approx. 2½ × 2¾in (6 × 7cm) of each

Matching sewing threads

Matching pastel stranded embroidery flosses (threads)

Blue ribbon, ⅝in (1.5cm) wide, 8in (20cm) long

Polyester stuffing

Needles, scissors, pins

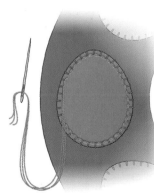

3 Cut a length of embroidery floss in a contrasting pastel color to the first egg and separate half the strands (so for six-stranded floss, use three strands). Using these strands and a larger needle if necessary, backstitch a line around the inside of the egg.

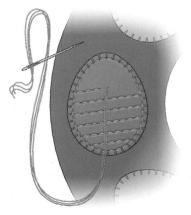

4 Decorate the egg with an embroidered pattern. Make a repeating pattern using simple stitches—copy the patterns pictured or design your own (see page 10 for some stitch inspiration). Embroider all the eggs, using a different pattern for each one. You may find it helpful to sketch the designs out on paper before you begin stitching, and to plan in advance which thread to use for each egg to ensure an even mix of colors around the wreath.

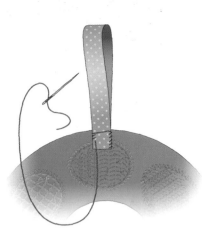

5 Fold the ribbon to make a loop and, with ¾in (2cm) overlapping the felt, whip stitch the ribbon ends to the top back of the wreath using matching blue sewing thread.

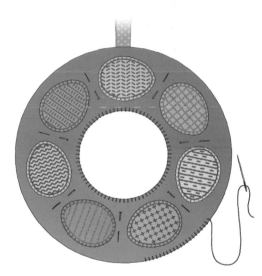

6 Pin the front and back of the wreath together, placing one pin in each gap between the eggs. Sew around the inside edge of the wreath using whip stitch and blue sewing thread. Then sew around the outside edge of the wreath with more whip stitches. Sew a section at a time, then remove the pins from around it (and set aside your needle) and stuff the section lightly with polyester stuffing. Then replace the pins if necessary and sew the next section. Repeat this until the whole wreath has been stuffed as evenly as possible, and the outside edge completely sewn.

birthday bunting

Layered bunting in pretty mix-and-match colors is a lovely decoration for birthday parties or other special occasions. The bunting pennants are made with an assortment of plain and patterned felt and lots of cute, colorful buttons. If you can't get hold of any patterned felt you could also use fabric, cutting the edges with pinking shears to help prevent fraying. If you want to use the bunting for year-round decoration, hang it out of direct sunlight.

1 Use the templates provided to cut out three pieces for each pennant: one plain felt scallop, one large pennant in another plain color, and one small patterned pennant. I used six patterns and six complementary plain colors, cutting out two of each shape required from each pattern and color to make twelve pennants in total. Cut as many pieces as you need for the length of bunting you want to make, spread out all the pieces on a table, and arrange them until you're happy with the combinations.

You will need:

Templates on page 125

Six pieces of patterned felt, approx. 4¾ × 7in (12 × 18cm) of each

Six pieces of felt in matching colors, approx. 8¼ × 8¾in (21 × 22cm) of each

Lots of pretty buttons in matching colors

Bias binding in a complementary color, 1in (2.5cm) wide, approx. 2yds (2m) long

Sewing thread to match the binding

Needle, scissors, pins

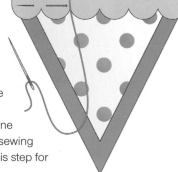

2 Make each pennant by pinning the three shapes together, aligning them at the top edge. Sew the three layers together with a line of running stitch along the top edge, using sewing thread to match the bias binding. Repeat this step for all the pennants you need for the bunting.

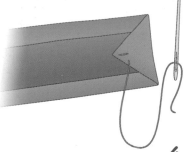

3 Cut a length of bias binding long enough to accommodate all the pennants, plus loops at each end. The bunting shown uses 2yds (2m) of bias binding, but if you want to add more pennants, or have larger spaces between the pennants, you'll need more binding. Fold the ends of the binding in to make a point and then fold this over. Sew the point down with a couple of stitches in matching thread, hiding the knot between the layers.

4 Fold the end of the binding in half lengthways and begin sewing it together with a line of neat running stitches close to the open edge. When you've sewn 6–8in (15–20cm), fold it over to make a loop. Sew the loop in place with a couple of stitches and sew on a large button to cover the join. You'll need to make an identical loop at the other end of the bunting, so make sure you leave enough at the end after sewing all the pennants in place.

5 One by one, sew all the pennants to the binding, spacing them about ¼in (5mm) apart. Fold the binding over the top edge of each pennant, pin or hold it in place, and sew along the edge of the binding with neat running stitches. Hide all the knots inside the binding and finish the stitches neatly on the back. When you've sewn on all the pennants, sew a loop to match the one at the other end and decorate it with another button to cover the join.

6 Decorate the binding with lots of buttons. Sew three buttons to the top of each pennant, using the scallops as a guide to spacing them evenly. Use doubled blue thread to match the binding, hiding the knots under the felt scallops. Sew a neat running stitch line between the three buttons as you sew them in position, then finish the stitching neatly on the back of the bunting.

bat ornaments

These bats would be a cute addition to your Halloween decorating. Just make one, or make a whole cloud of bats to hang all over the house. For extra spookiness, use white thread to add fangs and transform them into vampire bats! The wings need to be quite stiff, so use 100 percent wool felt, or thicker craft felt, or cut an extra layer or two if you're using thin felt.

1 Use the templates to cut out two black wing shapes, two dark gray body shapes, and two light gray ear shapes.

2 Pin the two wing pieces together. Cut a length of black embroidery floss and set aside half the strands (so for six-stranded floss, use three strands). Using the floss and a large needle, sew the wings together with running stitch, turning the wings over and back again as you sew to ensure the line is neat and straight on both sides. Sew the four dotted lines across the wings first, sewing along each line and then back again, and so filling in the gaps to create a continuous line of stitching. Then sew around the edge of the wings, finishing neatly on one side (this will be the back of the wings). Sewing black on black can be a bit tricky, so make sure you have good light to work by!

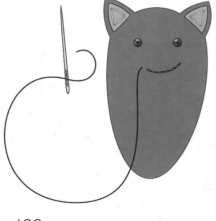

3 Place the two light gray ear shapes on one bat body piece. Sew them in position with a triangle of three stitches in light gray sewing thread. With black sewing thread, sew two black seed beads on as eyes (using three or four stitches per bead) and backstitch a curved smile. If you want to make vampire bats, make a few small stitches with white sewing thread to add two fangs to the smile.

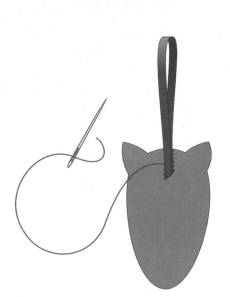

4 Fold the length of narrow black ribbon in half to form a loop and, with ⅜in (1cm) overlapping the felt, sew the ends to the top of the second bat body shape. Use whip stitches in dark gray sewing thread.

5 Arrange the two bat body shapes on the front and back of the wings (making sure the side of the wings where you finished the stitching is facing backward). Line the body shapes up carefully and pin all three layers together. Sew the layers together by stitching around the edge of the bat body with dark gray sewing thread and small running stitches. Turn the bat over and back again as you sew to ensure a neat line on both sides. Finish the stitches neatly on the back.

snow globe doorhanger

Traditional snow globes are one of the delights of the festive season. This felt version features an appliquéd winter scene, complete with a sprinkling of sparkly snow. Embroider a child's name on the base and hang it on their door over the holidays, or leave it blank and use the globe as an ornament in decorating your home.

1 Cut out all the pieces using the templates: cut a light blue globe, a red base, a brown reindeer, a dark green fir tree, white snowy ground, and a white snow cap for the tree.

2 Use straight stitches and matching threads to sew all the pieces in position one by one. Hold the larger pieces in place using pins and the smaller ones with your thumb and forefinger as you sew with the other hand. Sew the pieces in this order: first the blue globe to the black felt, then the white snowy ground at the bottom of the globe, then the fir tree sitting on top of the snow on the left. Next, the white cap of snow on top of the tree, then the reindeer in front of the tree, and finally the red base beneath the globe.

3 Use the two black seed beads for the reindeer's eyes. Use three or four stitches with black thread to sew them flat like an "O", with the holes visible in the center like pupils.

4 Position white sequins for falling snow over the scene in the snow globe, spacing them evenly and leaving the reindeer clear. Sew each sequin in place with white thread and three straight stitches.

5 Cut a length of silver embroidery floss and set aside half the strands. You may need to switch to a needle with a larger eye, and you may find it easier to sew with short lengths of floss at a time, as metallic floss is harder to work with than normal embroidery floss. With the silver thread, backstitch a line flush around the edge of the globe.

You will need:

Templates on page 126

Light blue felt, approx.
4½ × 4½in (11 × 11cm)

Red felt, approx. 2 × 4in
(5 × 10cm)

White felt, approx.
2 × 5in (5 × 13cm)

Brown felt, approx.
3 × 3½in (8 × 9cm)

Dark green felt, approx.
2½ × 2¾in (6 × 7cm)

Black felt, approx. 5½ × 9½in
(14 × 24cm)

Matching sewing threads

Two black seed beads, size 9/0

Fifteen white round sequins,
¼in (5mm) diameter

Narrow red ribbon,
8in (20cm)

Silver stranded
embroidery floss

Needles, scissors, pins

Pen

Small piece of greaseproof
paper or thin tracing paper

6 Draw around the base template with a pen onto a piece of greaseproof paper or thin tracing paper. Write the name you want to embroider in neat capitals in the center. Cut roughly around the drawn base and pin it over the base sewn on the snow globe.

7 With two strands of silver embroidery floss, carefully backstitch over the pencil letters using small, neat stitches. When you've finished stitching, carefully tear away the paper, using a pin to remove any small fiddly pieces.

8 Trim the black backing felt, cutting around the edge of the snow globe to leave a narrow black border all the way around. Then pin the snow globe to more black felt and use it as a template to cut out an identical backing piece.

9 Fold the ribbon into a loop. With ¾in (2cm) overlapping the felt, sew the ends to the top of the backing using black thread. Be careful the stitches don't show on the front. Pin the front and back together, with the ribbon ends between. Sew the pieces together with a line of black running stitch around the outer edge.

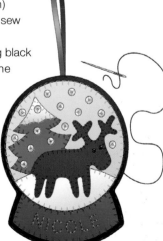

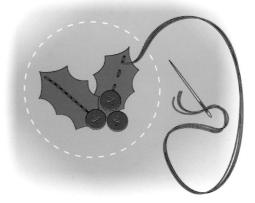

embroidery hoop ornaments

Two little felt pictures framed in mini wooden embroidery hoops—a crafty twist on classic baubles. Use felt that's not too thick for the background of your pictures, as you need to be able to stretch it in the hoop like fabric. For added detail, add sequins or mini buttons to embellish the holly or mistletoe berries.

1 Stretch a piece of bright green felt over the inner ring of the embroidery hoop. Place the outer ring of the hoop over the top and tighten the screw to close the hoop and hold the felt in place.

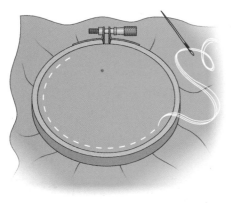

2 Cut a length of embroidery floss (white for the holly design, red for the mistletoe design) and set aside half the strands (so for six-stranded floss, use three strands). With a large needle, stitch a circle of small running stitches following the inside curve of the wooden hoop. Take the felt out of the hoop before you finish the stitching, then finish it neatly on the back. The stitched circle helps frame the design and acts as a guide for positioning the appliquéd pieces in the next stages.

3 Make a paper template by drawing around the inside of the inner ring of the hoop with a pencil. Cut this out and use it as a template to cut out one circle of bright green felt for each hoop ornament. Using the templates, cut out the leaf pieces from dark green felt: a sprig of mistletoe, or one large and one small holly leaf. Also cut out three small white circles or three small red circles to serve as berries (see page 8 for tips on cutting out small shapes).

4 Arrange the leaf and berry shapes in the center of the stitched circle. When you're happy with the arrangement, pin the leaves in place. Sew the berries in position with matching red or white embroidery floss (using half the strands, as before), sewing two small stitches to form a cross shape in the center of each berry.

5 With half the strands of dark green embroidery floss, sew a line down the center of each leaf to hold it in place. Make the line straight for the holly and curved for the mistletoe.

You will need:

Templates on page 126

Bright green felt, approx. 9 × 9in (23 × 23cm) for each ornament

Small pieces of red, white, and dark green felt

Red, white, and dark green stranded embroidery flosses (threads)

Ribbon, ¼in (5mm) wide, approx. 12in (30cm) long for each ornament

Embroidery hoop, 3in (8cm) diameter for each ornament

Fabric glue

Pencil and paper

Large needle, scissors, pins

6 Cut more red or white embroidery floss (to match the stitched circle), and sew around the edge of the motif with small running stitches.

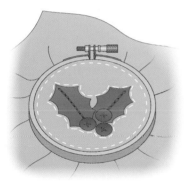

7 Put the design back in the hoop, lining up the circle with the ring, and making sure the closure is at the top. Then close the hoop tightly.

8 Turn the hoop over and trim off excess felt. Glue the circle cut in Step 3 to the back of the picture. Leave the hoop to dry, then tie a 12in (30cm) length of red or white ribbon to the hoop closure. Trim the ends at an angle to help prevent fraying.

gingerbread cookie garland

A string of yummy gingerbread cookies decorated with white felt frosting and a sprinkling of silver balls. Hang the garland across your mantelpiece or on your Christmas tree, or sew larger ribbon loops on each cookie to make a set of ornaments. If you can't find ginger felt, use brown felt instead and make a garland of traditional European spice biscuits instead of gingerbread cookies.

1 Using the templates, cut out all the shapes needed for the garland. For each gingerbread cookie you will need one white felt frosting shape (defined by the dotted line on the template) and two matching ginger felt cookie shapes.

2 Place one of the frosting shapes in the center of a matching cookie shape and pin it in position. Using white sewing thread, straight stitch around the edge of the frosting, then remove the pin. Repeat this for all the frosting shapes.

3 Sew lots of silver seed beads onto each cookie, as if they've been sprinkled at random onto the frosting. Use doubled white thread and one stitch through each bead. If you prefer, you could use seed beads in mixed pastel colors (to represent hundreds and thousands) instead of silver beads.

4 Cut a length of narrow ribbon for each cookie: if you're making a garland, cut 2¾in (7cm) lengths of ribbon, for ornaments cut 4–5in (10–13cm) lengths. I used a red and white gingham check ribbon, but you could use plain red ribbon or any other festive color. Fold the ribbon to make a loop and, with ⅜in (1cm) overlapping the felt, whip stitch the ribbon ends to the back of each frosted cookie. Sew through the ginger felt only, so that the stitches don't show on the front.

5 Pin the frosted front and plain back pieces of one cookie together and whip stitch around the edges with ginger sewing thread. Leave a small gap for stuffing the cookie, large enough to fit your finger through. Remove the pin.

6 Stuff each cookie lightly with polyester stuffing, using a pencil to poke the stuffing into all the small corners. Then whip stitch the gap closed, finishing the stitching neatly on the back.

7 Thread the cookies onto a long piece of ribbon, approximately 1½yds (1.5m) long, using silver jingle bells as spacers between the cookies. If you miss out the bell spacers you will require less ribbon. Leave gaps of about 3in (8cm) between each bell and cookie, and leave a 8–12in (20–30cm) plain length of ribbon at each end to tie the garland in place.

mitten ornaments

A set of cute ornaments embroidered to look like woolen mittens. I used red and blue with white stitching for a traditional look, but these would also look great in bright colors. Make a set of small mitten ornaments for your holiday tree, or large mittens that you can use like mini stockings. Use 100 percent wool felt or an acrylic felt that's thick enough to be embroidered without distorting the mitten.

1 For each ornament you want to make, use the template to cut out two mitten shapes from red or blue felt.

2 Cut a length of white embroidery floss and separate half the strands (so for six-stranded floss, use three strands). Using this floss and a large needle, decorate one of the mitten shapes. Backstitch a horizontal line where the cuff meets the body of the mitten, and a row of small vertical lines to create a ribbed effect. For the large mitten, sew an extra line across the top of the mitten cuff, joining the vertical lines together like the side of a ladder.

You will need:

Templates on page 127

Red and blue craft felt, approx. 3½ × 5½ (9 × 14cm) for each small mitten and approx. 4¾ × 8in (12 × 20cm) for each large mitten

Matching sewing threads

White stranded embroidery floss (thread)

Narrow red and blue ribbon, 4in (10cm) for each small mitten and 6in (15cm) for each large mitten

Needles, scissors, pins

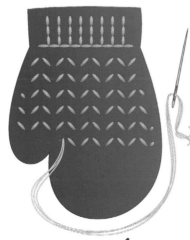

3 With more white embroidery floss (half the strands, as before), embroider the body of the mitten with a pattern of your choice. Make a repeating pattern using simple stitches—copy the patterns pictured or design your own (see page 10 for some stitch inspiration). You may find it helpful to sketch the design out on paper before you begin stitching. Use simple patterns for the small mittens, and experiment with more detailed patterns on the large mittens. Always leave a narrow border around the edge of the mitten, and where the pattern nears the edge, sew parts of it as if it continues on the other side. Finish the stitching neatly on the back and trim any loose threads.

4 Turn the decorated mitten over. Cut a length of narrow red or blue ribbon, 4in (10cm) for the small mittens, 6in (15cm) for the large mittens. Fold the ribbon over to form a loop and, with ⅜in (1cm) of ribbon overlapping the felt and using matching thread, whip stitch the ends to the top left of the mitten shape. Take care not to sew completely through the felt (if you have difficulty doing this, sew the ribbon to the plain backing mitten shape instead).

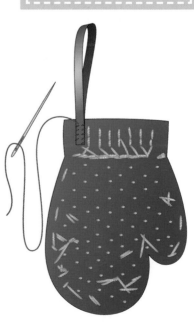

5 Pin the decorated front and plain back of the mitten together and sew them with white embroidery floss (using half the strands, as before). Sew around the edge and then back again with small running stitches to create a continuous line, turning the mitten over and back again as you sew to ensure the line is straight on both sides. Stitch completely around the small mittens, but leave the top of the large mittens open.

Templates

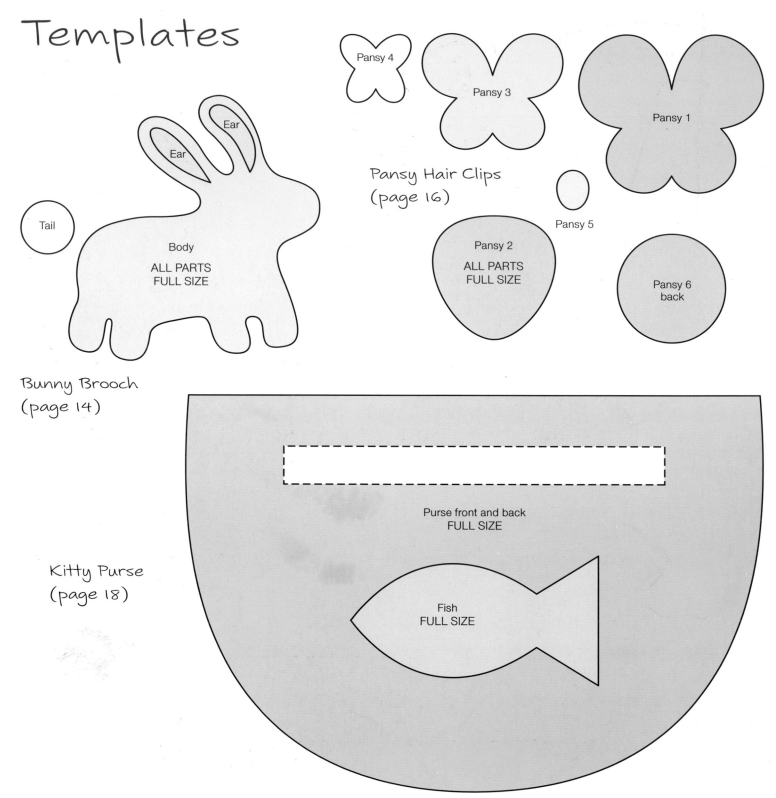

Pansy 4

Pansy 3

Pansy 1

Pansy Hair Clips
(page 16)

Pansy 5

Pansy 2
ALL PARTS
FULL SIZE

Pansy 6
back

Ear

Ear

Tail

Body
ALL PARTS
FULL SIZE

Bunny Brooch
(page 14)

Kitty Purse
(page 18)

Purse front and back
FULL SIZE

Fish
FULL SIZE

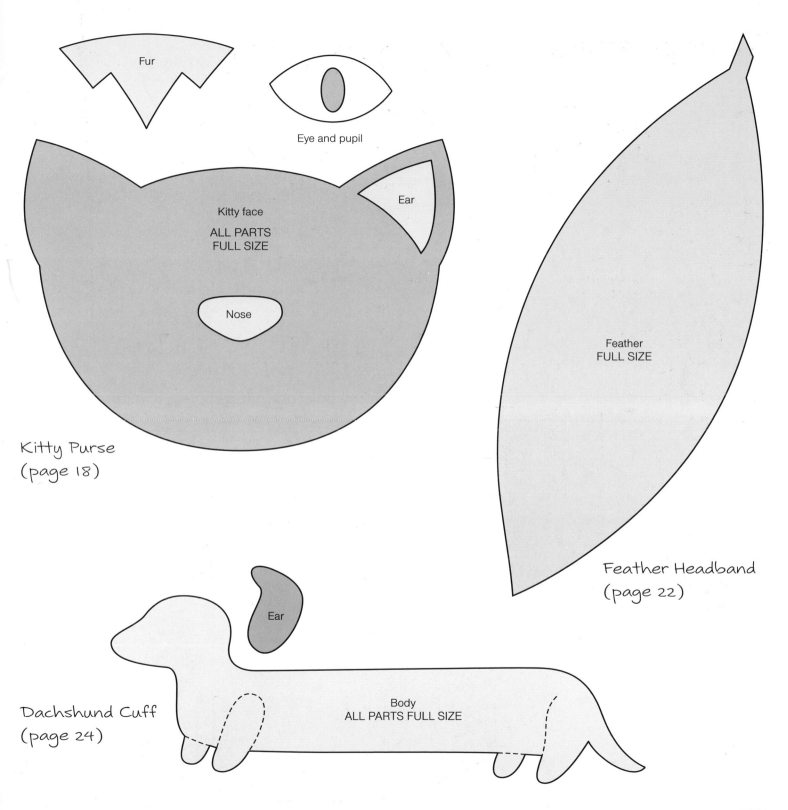

Fur

Eye and pupil

Kitty face
ALL PARTS
FULL SIZE

Ear

Nose

Kitty Purse
(page 18)

Feather
FULL SIZE

Feather Headband
(page 22)

Ear

Dachshund Cuff
(page 24)

Body
ALL PARTS FULL SIZE

Retro Corsage
(page 26)

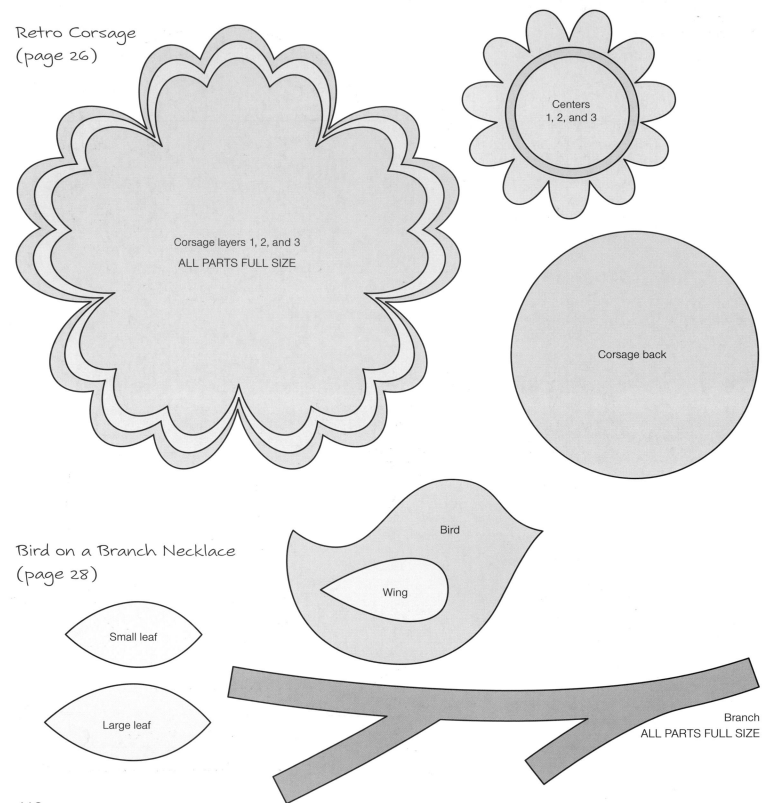

Centers
1, 2, and 3

Corsage layers 1, 2, and 3
ALL PARTS FULL SIZE

Corsage back

Bird on a Branch Necklace
(page 28)

Bird

Wing

Small leaf

Large leaf

Branch
ALL PARTS FULL SIZE

Sewing Brooch
(page 30)

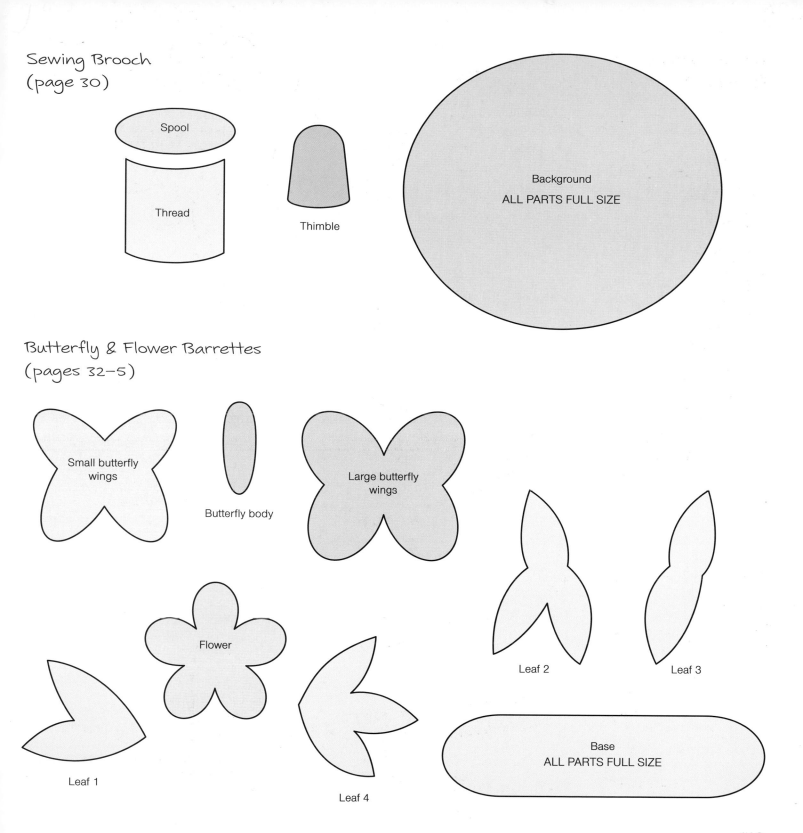

Spool

Thread

Thimble

Background
ALL PARTS FULL SIZE

Butterfly & Flower Barrettes
(pages 32–5)

Small butterfly
wings

Butterfly body

Large butterfly
wings

Leaf 2

Leaf 3

Flower

Leaf 1

Leaf 4

Base
ALL PARTS FULL SIZE

Hedgehog Phone Case (page 38)

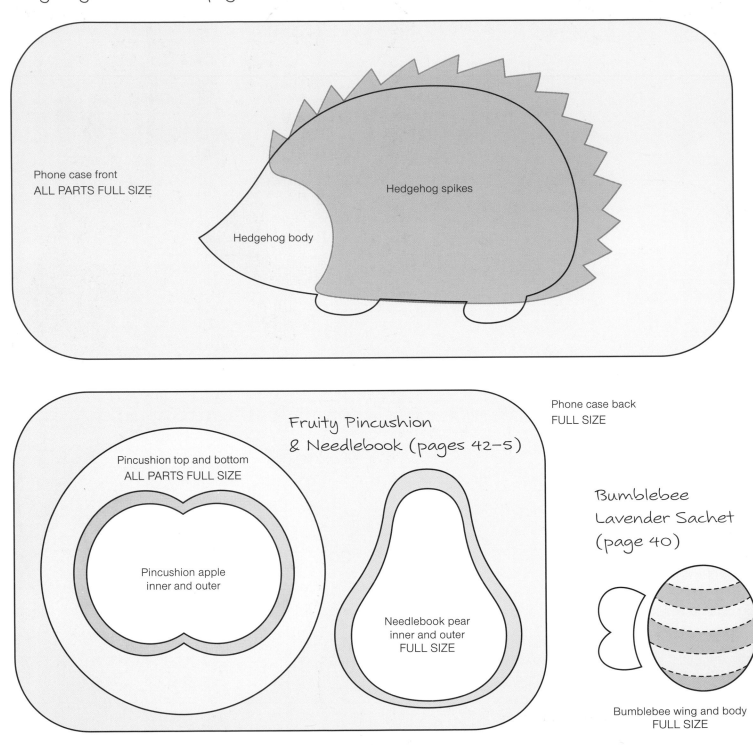

Phone case front
ALL PARTS FULL SIZE

Hedgehog spikes

Hedgehog body

Phone case back
FULL SIZE

Fruity Pincushion
& Needlebook (pages 42–5)

Pincushion top and bottom
ALL PARTS FULL SIZE

Pincushion apple
inner and outer

Needlebook pear
inner and outer
FULL SIZE

Bumblebee
Lavender Sachet
(page 40)

Bumblebee wing and body
FULL SIZE

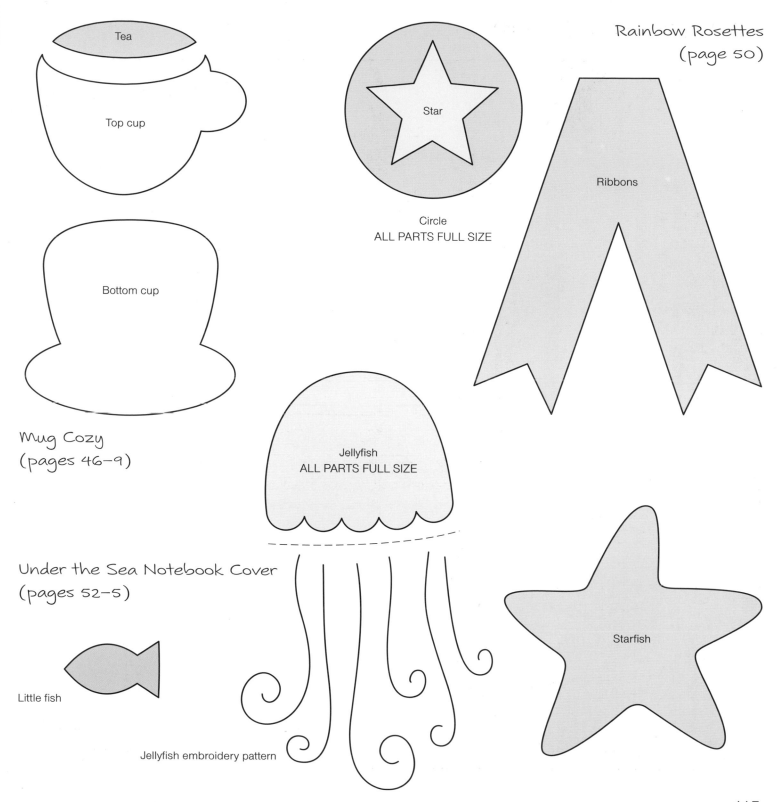

Tea

Top cup

Bottom cup

Star

Circle
ALL PARTS FULL SIZE

Rainbow Rosettes
(page 50)

Ribbons

Mug Cozy
(pages 46–9)

Jellyfish
ALL PARTS FULL SIZE

Under the Sea Notebook Cover
(pages 52–5)

Little fish

Jellyfish embroidery pattern

Starfish

Angel Teddy
(pages 56–9)

Muzzle

Ear

Face

Eye

Nose

Heart

Body
ALL PARTS FULL SIZE

Wings

Halo

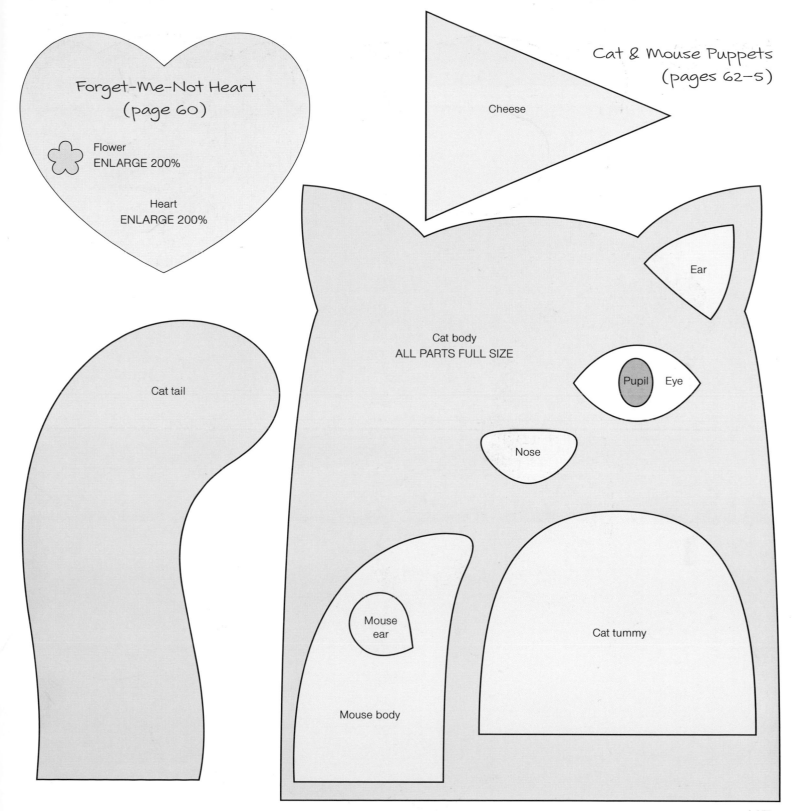

Forget-Me-Not Heart
(page 60)

Flower
ENLARGE 200%

Heart
ENLARGE 200%

Cheese

Cat & Mouse Puppets
(pages 62–5)

Ear

Cat body
ALL PARTS FULL SIZE

Pupil Eye

Cat tail

Nose

Mouse
ear

Cat tummy

Mouse body

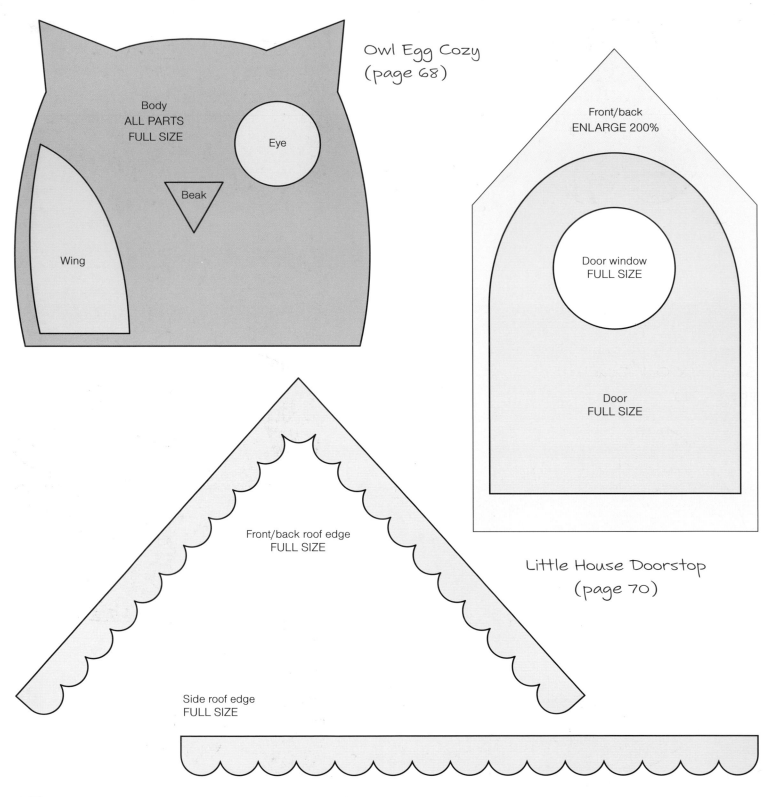

Owl Egg Cozy
(page 68)

Body
ALL PARTS
FULL SIZE

Eye

Beak

Wing

Front/back
ENLARGE 200%

Door window
FULL SIZE

Door
FULL SIZE

Little House Doorstop
(page 70)

Front/back roof edge
FULL SIZE

Side roof edge
FULL SIZE

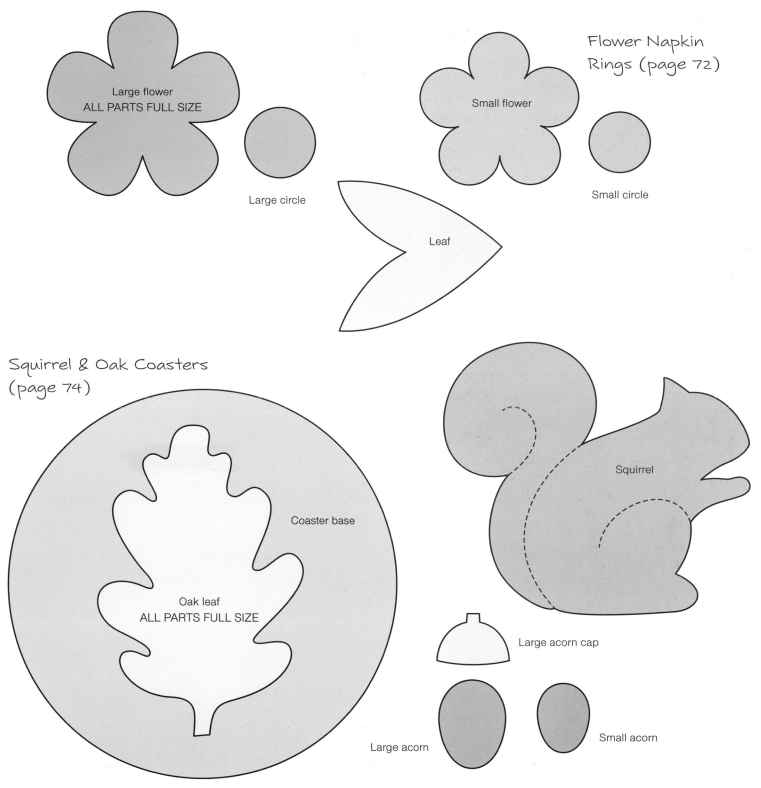

Flower Napkin
Rings (page 72)

Large flower
ALL PARTS FULL SIZE

Large circle

Small flower

Small circle

Leaf

Squirrel & Oak Coasters
(page 74)

Coaster base

Oak leaf
ALL PARTS FULL SIZE

Squirrel

Large acorn cap

Large acorn

Small acorn

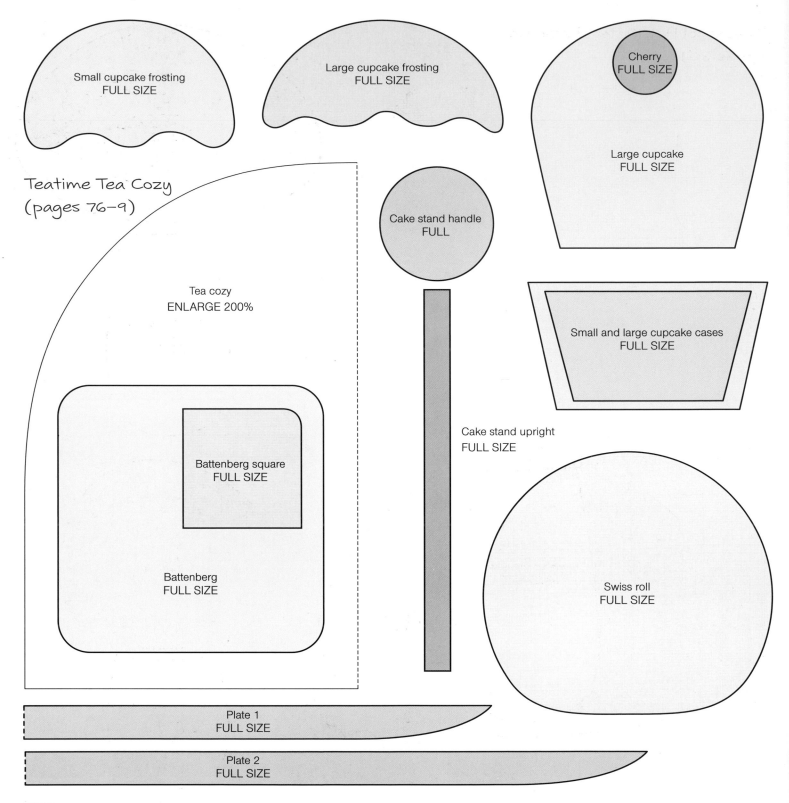

Small cupcake frosting
FULL SIZE

Large cupcake frosting
FULL SIZE

Cherry
FULL SIZE

Large cupcake
FULL SIZE

Teatime Tea Cozy
(pages 76–9)

Cake stand handle
FULL

Tea cozy
ENLARGE 200%

Small and large cupcake cases
FULL SIZE

Battenberg square
FULL SIZE

Cake stand upright
FULL SIZE

Battenberg
FULL SIZE

Swiss roll
FULL SIZE

Plate 1
FULL SIZE

Plate 2
FULL SIZE

Toadstool Hot Water Bottle Cover
(page 80)

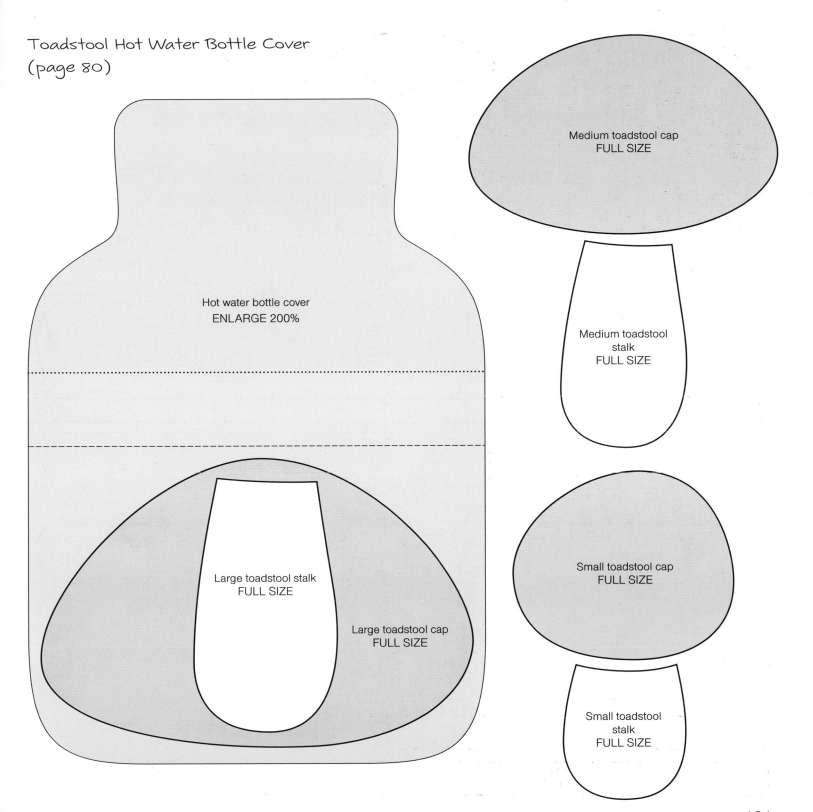

Hot water bottle cover
ENLARGE 200%

Large toadstool stalk
FULL SIZE

Large toadstool cap
FULL SIZE

Medium toadstool cap
FULL SIZE

Medium toadstool
stalk
FULL SIZE

Small toadstool cap
FULL SIZE

Small toadstool
stalk
FULL SIZE

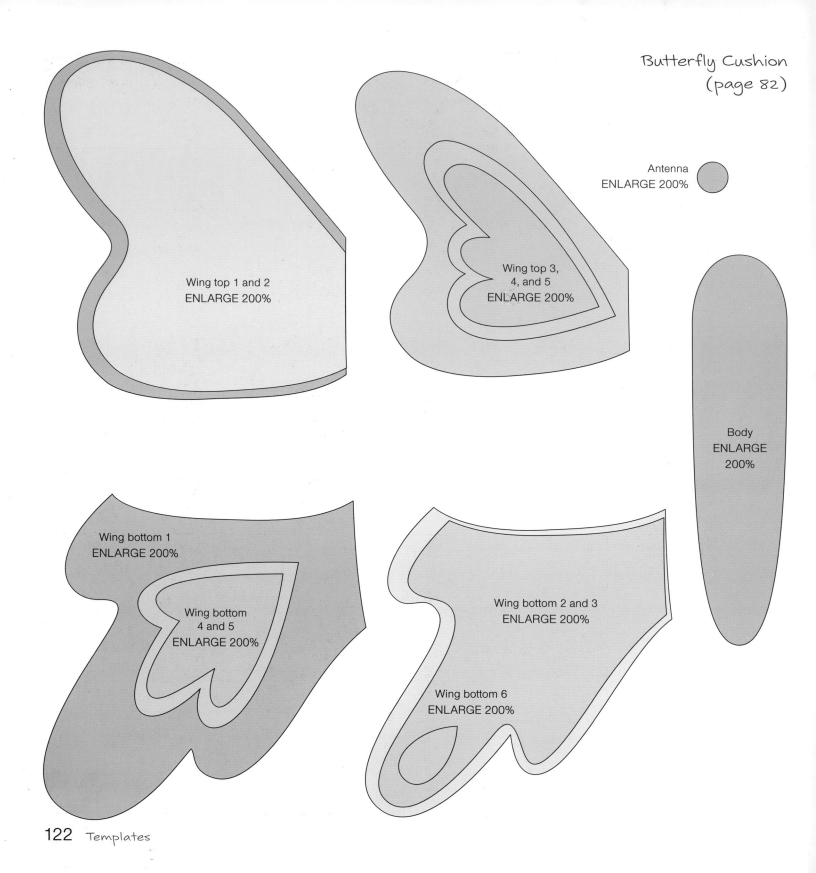

Butterfly Cushion
(page 82)

Antenna
ENLARGE 200%

Wing top 1 and 2
ENLARGE 200%

Wing top 3,
4, and 5
ENLARGE 200%

Body
ENLARGE
200%

Wing bottom 1
ENLARGE 200%

Wing bottom
4 and 5
ENLARGE 200%

Wing bottom 2 and 3
ENLARGE 200%

Wing bottom 6
ENLARGE 200%

Lovebirds Mobile
(page 84)

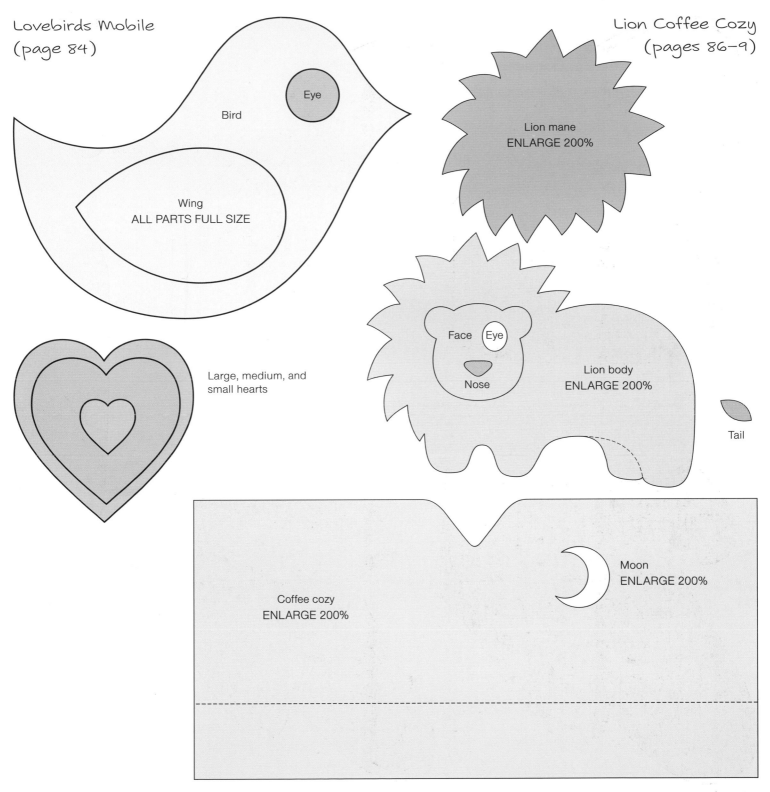

Eye

Bird

Wing
ALL PARTS FULL SIZE

Lion mane
ENLARGE 200%

Large, medium, and
small hearts

Face   Eye

Nose

Lion body
ENLARGE 200%

Tail

Moon
ENLARGE 200%

Coffee cozy
ENLARGE 200%

Templates 123

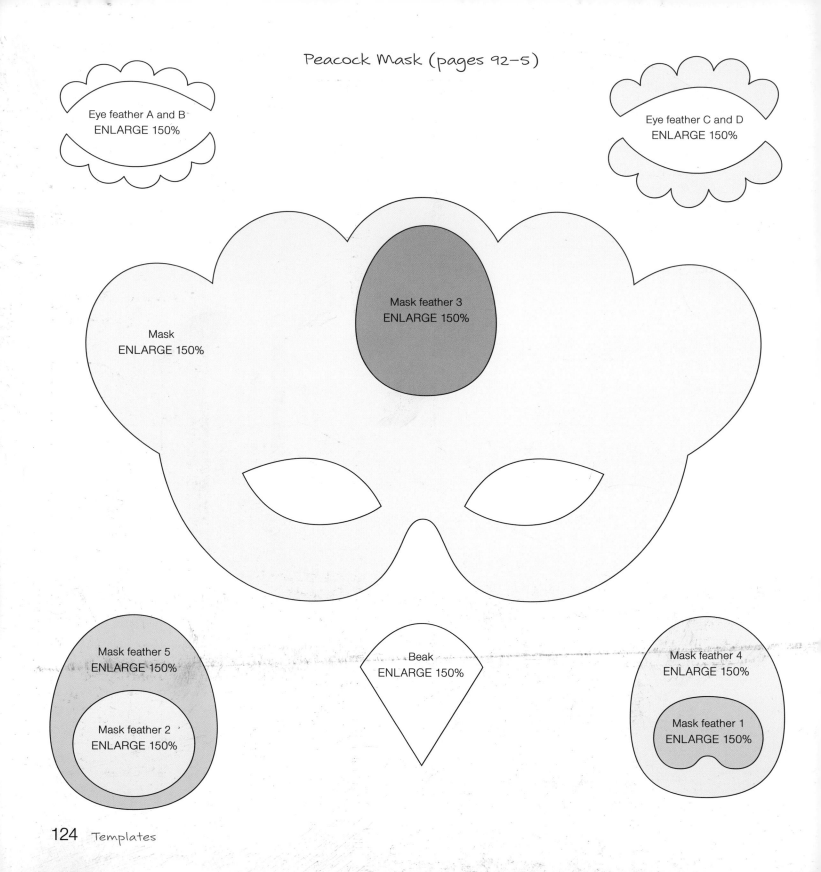

Peacock Mask (pages 92–5)

Eye feather A and B
ENLARGE 150%

Eye feather C and D
ENLARGE 150%

Mask feather 3
ENLARGE 150%

Mask
ENLARGE 150%

Mask feather 5
ENLARGE 150%

Mask feather 2
ENLARGE 150%

Beak
ENLARGE 150%

Mask feather 4
ENLARGE 150%

Mask feather 1
ENLARGE 150%

Easter Wreath
(page 96)

Wreath
ENLARGE 200%

Egg
ENLARGE
200%

Birthday Bunting
(page 98)

Small and large pennants
ALL PARTS FULL SIZE

Scalloped trim

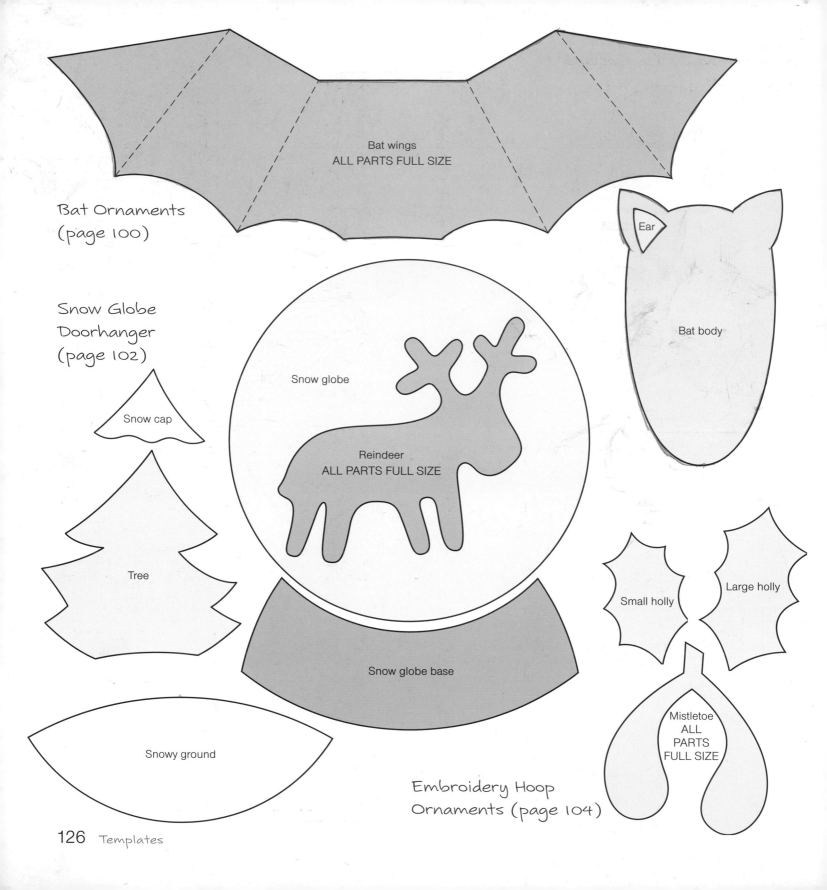

Bat wings
ALL PARTS FULL SIZE

Bat Ornaments
(page 100)

Ear

Bat body

Snow Globe
Doorhanger
(page 102)

Snow cap

Snow globe

Reindeer
ALL PARTS FULL SIZE

Tree

Small holly

Large holly

Snow globe base

Snowy ground

Mistletoe
ALL
PARTS
FULL SIZE

Embroidery Hoop
Ornaments (page 104)

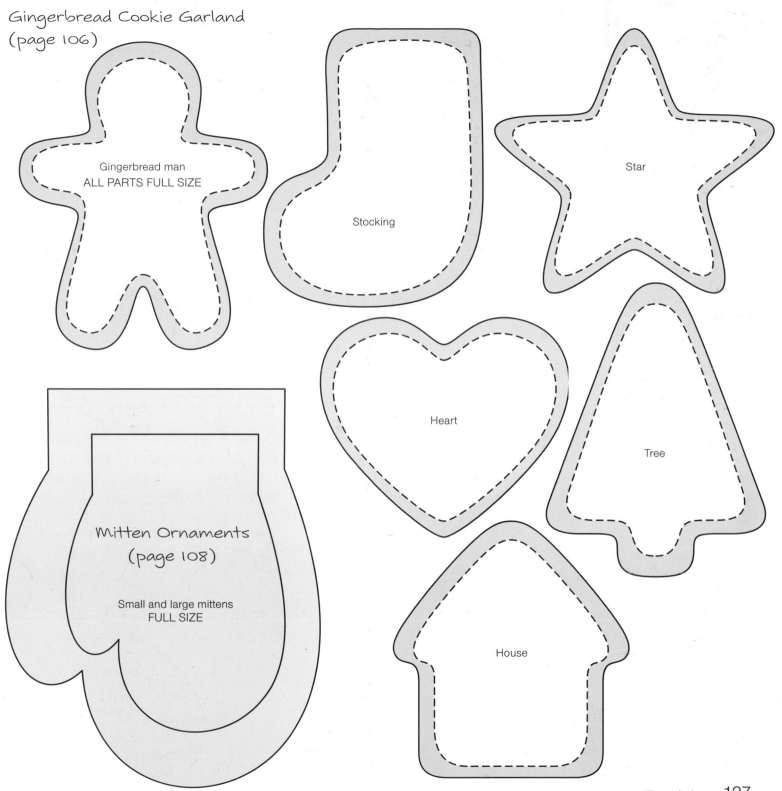

Gingerbread Cookie Garland
(page 106)

Gingerbread man
ALL PARTS FULL SIZE

Stocking

Star

Heart

Tree

Mitten Ornaments
(page 108)

Small and large mittens
FULL SIZE

House

Suppliers

USA

A Child's Dream Come True
www.achildsdream.com

American Felt and Craft
www.feltandcraft.com

Benzie Design
www.benziedesign.com

Hobby Lobby
www.hobbylobby.com

Joann Fabric & Craft Stores
www.joann.com

Michaels
www.michaels.com

Purl Soho
www.purlsoho.com

Weir Crafts
www.weircrafts.com

UK

Beads Unlimited
www.beadsunlimited.co.uk

Blooming Felt
www.bloomingfelt.co.uk

Cloud Craft
www.cloudcraft.co.uk

Fabric Land
www.fabricland.co.uk

Fred Aldous
www.fredaldous.co.uk

Hobbycraft
www.hobbycraft.co.uk

John Lewis
www.johnlewis.com

Myriad Natural Toys & Crafts
www.myriadonline.co.uk

Paper-And-String
www.paper-and-string.net

The Eternal Maker
www.eternalmaker.com

Index